Peru under the Incas

LIFE IN ANCIENT LANDS
Edited by Edward Bacon

*Peru
under the Incas*

C. A. Burland

Evans Brothers Limited London

© George Rainbird Ltd 1967

First published 1967

This book was designed and produced by George Rainbird Ltd
2 Hyde Park Place, London W2,
for Evans Brothers Limited,
Montague House, Russell Square, London WC1.
7/5053
The text was filmset in Great Britain by
Cox and Sharland Ltd, Southampton.
The book was printed and bound in Hungary.

67- 114040

CONTENTS

COLOUR PLATES

FOREWORD

The world as we know it is a man-made world. Hardly any part of the habitable globe is unaffected by man's activity; even some of the parts which are uninhabitable were made so by man. And man himself is very largely a man-made creature: his habits, his thoughts, his memory, his aspirations are the modified sum of his ancestors' experiences.

All men are brothers, say the missionary and the idealist. True, but there is more to it than that: all men, living and dead since the beginning of time, are our brothers; and all history is family history. The Magdalenian artist of 17,000 years ago who decorated the caves of Lascaux with bulls and horses, the Cretan who applauded the bull-leapers, the Egyptian who drew funny hippopotamuses on pieces of stone, the boy Inca who triumphed in the initiation tests, the Etruscans who delighted so frankly in wine, women and song — these are as real to us, as near to us and as sustaining to us as, at any rate, some of those who live in our own street, village, town. Or they can be.

Aristotle said that the object of poetry was pleasure. And when he used these words, he doubtless used them in the widest possible sense: poetry, to include the full range of man's creative imagination; pleasure, to encompass everything from the baby's first chuckle to the philosopher's cry of delight at apprehending a new facet of truth. Education and the pursuit of knowledge have two objectives: pleasure and power. And of these the greater is pleasure: power is transitory, pleasure is permanent.

If these books enable anyone to pass an examination, to secure a job or to dominate a competitor or friend, they will have served a purpose of a sort. Their main objective, however, is to increase the sum of human pleasure, to enlarge the circle of friendship, love and knowledge, and to present a picture of life.

More than most vanished civilizations the world of the Incas speaks directly to us today. They did so many things so well: they ordered their society so firmly and justly — "from each according to his powers, to each according to his needs" — they built such splendid roads in such impossible country, their communication system was such a marvel despite their ignorance of the wheel and their lack of any form of writing, they were brilliant agriculturalists, they were the very model of a planned economy — and yet they fell to pieces irretrievably at the first hint of disunion and the first approach of a handful of Spaniards.

They are the especial pride of economists, social organizers, planners — the people who increasingly rule our lives today; and it is to our immediate advantage to know what life was like for the Andean Peruvians under the Inca rule before we nervelessly let the Incas of today take us over.

EDWARD BACON

INTRODUCTION

Young Prince Tupac was the only leading member of the Inca family to win the annual races and endurance trials held for Peruvian boys on reaching the age of fourteen. He was destined by his birth to become the Sapa Inca, divine ruler of the empire called Tahuantinsuyu, the Land of the Four Directions, so his unusual achievement in youth presaged well for the future. And so it was. This great man who took the title of Topa

Topa Inca Yupanqui, the Tenth Inca

Inca Yupanqui lived and ruled wisely. At the age of eighty-five he died, chanting a poem which compared his life to the blossoming and fading of a flower. The year was 1493. Christopher Columbus had already made his first landing in the West Indies. Yet it was to be another thirty years before the Spaniards in Darien heard a rumour of the Golden Empire to the south. The great Topa Yupanqui therefore faded from this world to live in the paradise of the Sun with no knowledge of the domestic tragedies and then the total subversion of the Inca family which were to befall.

In this book we shall glimpse his land, and try to make some estimate of the cultural achievements of his people and his family. It is not an easy journey for us. There were records kept on knotted cords which we can no longer read; there are stone walls, pottery vessels and the remains of roads. Best of all the wise men of Peru treasured the tales of their great leaders, and recited them to the Spaniards who recorded them with various degrees of prejudice. On the other hand, in the first generation after the disaster, descendants of the Inca family remembered their maternal ancestors and sought out information which enabled them to write the story with a pro-Inca bias. What develops from the study is an account of wonders which can be summed up in the name of the sun temple in Cuzco—Ccoricancha, the House of Gold.

Chapter One

THE LAND AND ITS INHABITANTS

The land of the Incas was not coincident with modern Peru. It included parts of Ecuador, the whole of Peru, the whole of Bolivia, and Chile as far south as the Maule river. Its eastern boundary was undefined but held within striking distance of a line of stone forts built on the fringes of the great tropical forests of Amazonia.

The shape of the land was determined, long before mankind arrived on the scene, by a series of tremendous upheavals of sedimentary rocks, which were eventually pushed more than four miles above the level of the ocean in which they were formed. The great throes of earth building were accompanied by uprushes of igneous rocks which sometimes solidified as great masses of granite, basalt and porphyry, and at other places burst through as volcanoes which surrounded themselves with lava fields and deserts of ash. The great mountains eventually formed a complex double chain throughout the region. Glaciers carved out steep valleys which were trenched deeper in later times by mountain torrents. But the winds nearly always blew in from the steamy Amazon jungles in the east to deposit their moisture as they swept up the Andean cordillera. Thus Peru achieved its geographical form before history began. Today it presents a picture of heavily forested eastern mountains, a region of high, chilly and moderately moist plateaus (plate 1), and dry western slopes leading down to a tropically hot desert coast watered only by short turbulent rivers crashing through the mountain barriers from the plateaus.

The shore was washed by a cold Antarctic current, often foggy and always full of fish. It is one of the richest fishing areas of the world. The rocks were the homes of great herds of seals and sea-lions, and of myriads of seabirds: terns, frigate birds, and pelicans. So the desolation of the desert land was compensated by the abundance of the sea.

The land was the home of many lizards and serpents; remarkable insects, often beautiful and sometimes dangerous, and a fauna which includes mice and rats, monkeys, pumas, jaguars, guinea pigs, and the varieties of the llama which flourished unpredictably on the desolate high plateau of the puna. The coastlands also sheltered wild deer in considerable numbers. The birds inland included the parrots and macaws of the Amazon forest, mountain hawks and eagles and the magnificent condor. Vegetation promised much for the days when man should come upon the scene; there were beans, and gourds, the quinoa grass with its rich clusters of seeds, and, most remarkable of all, the potato. Maize reached Peru only after man had been in the country for a long time.

Mankind probably reached Peru more than twenty thousand years ago. At some remote period their long forgotten ancestors had crossed from Siberia into Alaska, and through long ages had found their way, following the animals and fish upon which they lived, into the southern continent. They were the usual American Indian admixture of

11

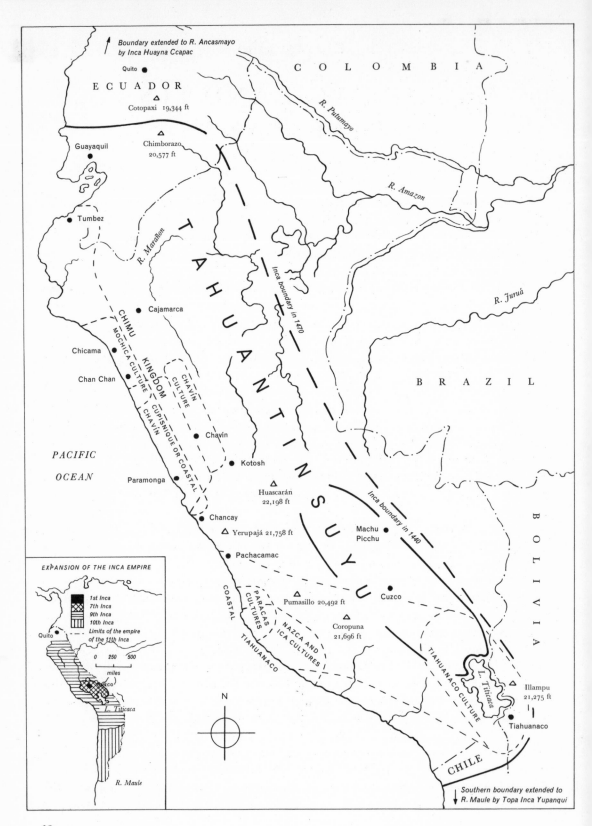

Boundary extended to R. Ancasmayo
by Inca Huayna Ccapac

Quito

C O L O M B I A

E C U A D O R

Cotopaxi 19,344 ft

R. Putumayo

Chimborazo
20,577 ft

Guayaquil

R. Amazon

Tumbez

R. Juruá

T A H U A N T I N S U Y U

R. Marañon

Inca boundary in 1470

Cajamarca

B R A Z I L

Chicama

CHIMU

Chan Chan

MOCHICA CULTURE

KINGDOM

CHAVÍN
CULTURE

Chavín

CUPISNIQUE OR COASTAL

Kotosh

CHAVÍN

PACIFIC

OCEAN

Paramonga

Huascarán
22,198 ft

Inca boundary in 1440

B O L I V I A

Chancay

Yerupajá 21,758 ft

Machu
Picchu

Pachacamac

EXPANSION OF THE INCA EMPIRE

COASTAL

PARACAS
CULTURES

Pumasillo 20,492 ft

Cuzco

1st Inca
7th Inca
9th Inca
10th Inca
Limits of the empire
of the 11th Inca

Quito

0   250   500

miles

NAZCA AND
ICA CULTURES

Coropuna
21,696 ft

Cuzco

TIAHUANACO CULTURE

L. Titicaca

Illampu
21,275 ft

L. Titicaca

TIAHUANACO

Tiahuanaco

R. Maule

N

CHILE

Southern boundary extended to
R. Maule by Topa Inca Yupanqui

12

Prehistoric Peruvians

peoples, rather short, and golden skinned, though some of the mountain peoples were quite a dark copper hue. All had straight black hair, but very little developed on their bodies and chins. They all had some Mongoloid characteristics, including the typical fold of the eyelid, and the typically fine grained, rather thick, skins. These tribes who marched on to the high plateaus must have found it hard to acclimatize, but eventually they withstood the low air pressures and brilliant light, as successfully as their coastal neighbours withstood the dry heat and denser air of sea level.

In the earliest times one must imagine the people of Peru were organized as quite small groups of fishermen and hunters. Various tribes probably spoke several distinct languages. When agriculture began, about seven thousand years ago, it became possible for the tribes to settle in fixed villages near their plantations. Only after this is it possible for the archaeologist to note the development of differences between the cultures of the settlements. About 1600 B.C. stone buildings were erected at Kotosh, but it was only about 900 B.C., when already the civilizations of the Old World were ancient, that the first high culture appeared in Peru. This occurred on the high plateau in the valley of the Marañon before it turns through the mountains to make its plunge into the Amazon forests. In this valley at least nine settlements with stone buildings have been found, of which the most famous is Chavín de Huantar.

Chavín art is apparently devoted to religious adoration of spirits of serpent and puma. It has an unmistakable quality of its own. Not long after its appearance in the mountains, this culture appeared on the Peruvian coast near the site of Cupisnique, where the characteristic art style is found in hand-moulded pottery. Some fragments of Chavín type pottery have recently been reported from the lower country where the Andes sink into the Amazonian forest. This is the first ceramic type to occur among a long series of potsherds which show that the linkage between the mountain and forest areas extended over the whole history of the higher cultures in Peru.

On the Peruvian coast in the beginnings of the Christian era, two other cultures arose. There was the culture of Nasca in the south, which has some features such as head hunting, and the use of clubs with a stone axe blade inserted midway in the length, which characterize forest tribes such as the Jivaro in recent times. In the north a very different but highly advanced culture arose in the fertile valleys which pierced the desert. This was formerly called Proto-Chimu, but when it was realized that it could have little to do with the later Chimu kingdoms of the same area it was renamed after the linguistic stock which inhabited the region, the Mochica . . . the people who spoke the Muchik language. The Nasca culture was overwhelmed and the Mochica crippled by an irruption of the people from the highland site of Tiahuanaco, which stands beside Lake Titicaca in Bolivia. Tiahuanaco art bears a relationship to the ancient Chavín style, but it is much later in time, and its domination of the coastal cultures must have occurred quite as late as the eighth and ninth centuries A.D.

The domination of Tiahuanaco was short-lived. Why it collapsed we do not know. On the southern coast it was succeeded by a number of minor cultures, and the Nasca civilization never revived. On the northern coasts there was a great revival of culture. The legends tell us of the arrival by sea of a great chief known as the Grand Chimu who with his courtiers and nobles united many cities and established an empire which was contemporary with the earlier Inca rulers in the highlands. In many ways the Chimu culture with its abundance of precious metals and groups of cities scattered along the coast north and south of the great capital city of Chan Chan exceeded the power of the earlier Incas. But it was a luxury-loving culture, and when the Inca decided it must become part of their empire of Tahuantinsuyu the resistance was slight, and the acceptance of Inca rule was the easy way.

The Spanish chronicler Montesinos gives us a list of "Amautas", or wise men, as he calls them, who were ancestral to the Incas. These cover an immense period of time, but so far there is little reason for giving credence to the story, though it may indicate that there was a traditional history going back to the beginnings of civilization in the Andean region.

It is becoming more and more apparent that the eastern slopes of the Andes were closely linked with the higher cultures of the plateau, in Chavín, Tiahuanaco and Inca times. Wherever the forest has been cleared, small fortresses, cultivation terraces and

14

Above. The Gate of the Sun at Tiahuanaco, rear view

Below. Chan Chan, the Chimu capital (photographed in 1931; torrential rain in 1934 destroyed much of what is shown here)

traces of roads have been found. In most of the sites pottery of all periods has been found. Thus there is less difficulty in accepting the idea of Montesinos that the Incas were in some way successors to previous dynasties who ruled in the high plateau regions. The archaeological record also tends to solve the problem posed by the Incas' own story of the arrival of the first members of their divine family from the east.

After Tiahuanaco rule had collapsed in the coastal regions of Peru it persisted in the highlands. Archaeology shows that the old strength of artistic design gradually becomes enfeebled and uncertain. Basic ceramic forms continue, but they are no longer associated with great monuments, only with the hill forts which bespeak of an unsettled world of constant raiding between different tribal groups. This has been called the Pucara, or hill fortress, culture.

Throughout the period of the decadent Pucara culture the Inca family was gathering strength. The family legend tells of the first Inca and his brothers coming over the eastern cordillera of the Andes. They carried a wedge of gold, the symbol of a sun ray, for they had been sent out by their father Inti, the Sun God, to found an empire which should bring peace to the Four Directions on Earth, to Tahuantinsuyu. They had been commanded to begin their rule from the place where the magic piece of gold should sink into the earth. Fabulous adventures changed all but the Inca Manco Ccapac and his sister into rocks or animals. Then came the day when this first Inca couple reached the Navel of the Earth, the Cuzco itself. Here on a level piece of ground they laid the wedge of gold, and it at once sank out of sight. This then was to become the centre of Tahuantinsuyu. Already there was a small town there, and the first of the Incas soon became a chieftain, ruling over just half the town, Hurin-Cuzco. In such a small way were great things begun. This adventure was not a far distant event, but purports to be an occurrence of the eleventh century A.D.

The first two Inca rulers seem to have ruled only in Hurin-Cuzco. They are so involved with mystery stories that there is uncertainty about the real nature of their existence. Manco Ccapac was succeeded by Sinchi (or Chief) Roca. That is about the extent of fact, but the remainder has great significance in that we are shown the Incas as a family of divine descent who began their dynasty in a small way with the rule of a section of a city. It was the lower section, near the flat ground where the golden wedge had sunken. The third Inca was Lloque Yupanqui. He ruled over no more territory, but was an organizer whose son, Mayta Ccapac, ruled all of the city of Cuzco and conquered one of the tribes of the nearby valley. His son was Ccapac Yupanqui who formed an alliance with the Andahuaylas, the most powerful tribe of the region. The successor was Inca Roca who began a struggle to overthrow the Chanca Confederacy. His bravery led only to a stalemate, and his son was the unfortunate Inca Yahuar Huaccac who was heavily defeated by the Chancas. Cuzco was nearly lost, and the unlucky Inca seems to have been disposed of. He was succeeded by Inca Viracocha who was named for the Supreme Creator. His skill and wisdom saved the situation and the Inca armies extended their rule over the whole of the highland plateau as far south as the ancient city of Tiahuanaco on Lake Titicaca. He assumed the title of Sapa Inca, The Only (or supreme) Inca.

It was the ninth Inca, Pachacutec, who broke out from the plateau. His armies stormed into the central coast near the ancient holy place of Pachacamac. They took over the

16

Platé 1. The high *puna* at Salinas, three miles above the sea. *Photo: Victor von Hagen*

Plate 2. Sacsahuaman, "Eyrie of Hawks", the stone fortress constructed by the Inca to defend Cuzco. The corner stones of the defensive terraces are twice the height of a man
Photo: Miss G. Farnell

DATES A.D.	PERU	NORTH AMERICA	EUROPE
950	End of Tiahuanaco power	End of Maya highland cities	Emperor Otto I
1000		Fall of Toltecs Vikings settle in Vinland	
			King Canute
	Incas settle in Cuzco		
1050		Mixtec conquests	
			Norman conquest of England
1100	Arrival of Chimu kings on coast		First Crusade
1150		Toltec-Chichimec rule at Tula	
			Emperor Barbarossa
1200	Incas control whole Cuzco valley		
			Magna Carta
1250	Inca expansion begins		Thomas Aquinas
1300			Dante Alighieri
	Inca Roca, first Sapa Inca	Aztecs found Tenochtitlán	
1350	Defeat of Yahuar Huaccac Inca Viracocha		Geoffrey Chaucer
		Moctecuzoma I founds Aztec Empire	
1400			
	Inca Pachacutec		Battle of Agincourt
1450		Period of Hiawatha	Turks capture Constantinople
	Topa Inca Yupanqui		
1500		Moctecuzoma II	Christopher Columbus discovers America
	Inca Huayna Ccapac	Fall of Mexico	
	Inca Atahuallpa	to Spaniards	
1550	Spanish power in Peru		

great Paramonga fortress and threatened the fabulously wealthy kingdom of the Chimu. The Chimu king put up a token resistance, but having learned how the Incas treated their enemies he made a formal surrender. The Chimu nobles had to surrender their wonderful golden ornaments to the Sun temple in Cuzco, and the king became a vassal of the Inca. However his conquerers sent an Inca princess to marry him, so that his children could rule the country as viceroys of true Inca descent.

The tenth Inca was the great Tupac Yupanqui. He inherited a rich empire, which he proceeded to enlarge by wars across the desert coasts into Chile, and campaigns into the great Amazon forests. In his day the Inca Empire was secure and powerful. That is the reason for our selection of the period for this book.

After Tupac Yupanqui came his son, the gentler Huayna Ccapac, who fell in love with a princess of the Cara people of Ecuador. At his death it was clear that he had divided his kingdom between his true heir, Huascar, and the son of his princess, the ferocious Atahuallpa who, after he had murdered his brother, fell victim to the Spanish invaders.

There was little risk of real hunger in the Inca dominions. The organization of the road system with its government storehouses for the army provided reserves which were made available to the populace on any occasion of local shortages. Through the storage

Plate 3. Gown of a nobleman of the Chimu kingdom, subjugated by the Inca. The outer pattern represents pelicans, the inner section shows the monkey-like form of the moon-crowned Sí, the principal deity of the Chimu. *Miss Kemper Collection. Photo: Derrick E. Witty*

depots there was a considerable interchange of foods and cloth from different regions of the country. Nevertheless the storehouses of the Inca were not primarily intended to improve local dietaries. The social organization was keyed to local self-sufficiency, and every community was expected to produce all its own local needs together with a good surplus for the storehouses of the Sun God, and the more accessible storehouses of the Inca.

Agriculture was highly organized. It was based on irrigation and soil conservation as far as possible. In the mountain regions, terraces edged by stone walls were constructed right down any accessible slopes, however steep (plate 12). Earth was sometimes carried to fill the terraces. These were watered by mountain streams which had been diverted into a system of stone-lined ditches. There was little need to allocate water to the individual fields of mountain villagers. However, the village elders always had ready a system of regulation which would allow the field holders to divert the stream over their land in strict rotation. This was arranged as an attempt to avoid quarrels, but in this they do not appear to have been overly successful.

In the hot coastal regions water was far more precious. The fields, which could be created only in the narrow ribbons of alluvial soil beside the rivers, were cultivated and cared for with the industry displayed by peasant farmers all over the world where cultivation is difficult. The shallow gradients of the coastal streams were characterized by wide meanders and oxbows. It was fairly simple to divert some of the water at the higher levels into narrow canals which ran along the fringes of the coastal desert. No cultivable land was neglected, and no buildings were permitted on land where food could be grown. However, in ancient times the desert cities were not so desolate as one would imagine. Many house blocks had sunken ponds, and sufficient earth and plant humus was conserved to grow flowers and pepper and spices for the home.

The basic tool of the farmer was the digging-stick. It was a stick about five feet long and as thick as one could grasp easily. A little way from the top a handle was lashed on so that one could push it down more easily, and to give still more power and leverage the pointed end of the stick was topped by a lashed-on pedal which was used to exert strong pressure from the digger's foot. The point of the stick was frequently shod with a bronze chisel-like blade which reduced wear and improved efficiency.

The village community divided the land among its members, and the head men of each ten families formed committees to regulate the apportionment both of land and of produce. They were responsible for selecting the proper amounts of the crops to be taken to the local town by the village headman for registration by the Quipucamayoc as the village contribution to the stores of Inti the Sun God, and the Lord Sapa Inca Tupac Yupanqui.

There was a division of labour. The men did the heavy digging, the women the fruitful planting. Children were busy weeding, and driving away birds and small animals. Most warriors first learned to use a sling when they were little boys scaring away birds. Most women had first learned to use a spindle when they were walking with their mothers to and from the fields. At this level the social organization was the natural order of things. Each member of a family used his natural abilities to help on the welfare of the whole. Each family was fully aware that they depended on their neighbours for extra help from time to time, and they willingly gave theirs in turn.

20

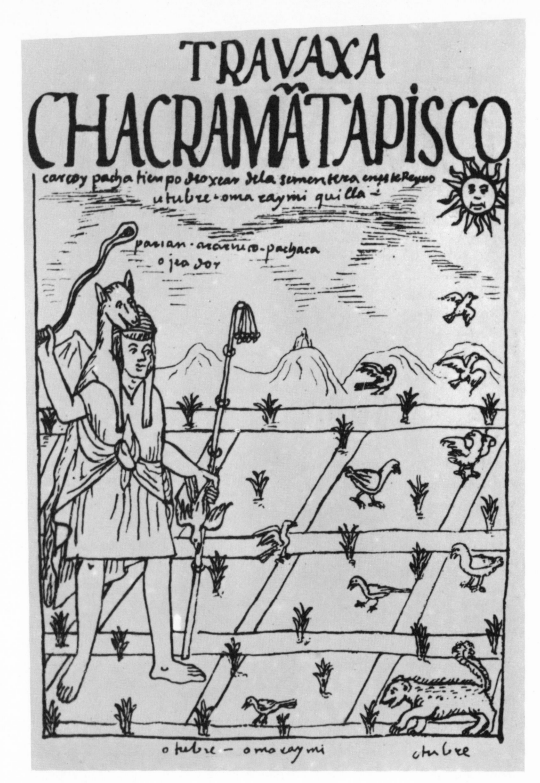

An irrigated field

The Quipucamayoc

22

The planting of the fields was a communal enterprise of great religious importance. On the appropriate festival day the Holy Sapa Inca himself went to a plot of land in Cuzco and made the first stab into the soil with a golden digging-stick. His sister-queen, the Ccoya, put the maize seed into the hole and smoothed the soil back by a pretty sweep of her sandal. Then every noble, and every village headman throughout Tahuantinsuyu, would perform the same sacred act. Everywhere the lines of villagers would work across their fields, digging and planting while singing festival songs to the gods. Ploughing day was a day to wear one's best clothes and have some flowers in one's hair. Mankind had made the earth magically pregnant and rejoiced that Rainbow, Sun and Thunder would bring the work to a happy fruition.

The maize plant was the staple food of the Peruvian Indians. For more than two thousand years they had cultivated it, but we now know that its origins lay in Mexico some two millennia earlier. It took a long time to penetrate the southern continent, but everywhere that it was grown it came to be regarded as the kindly mother of food.

Quinoa, which is an excellent grain for the highland areas and able to grow above the level of the maize fields, was an older grain in Peru.

Potatoes were also a rich source of starch. The Peruvian Indians had cultivated potatoes, which were native to their country, for so long that they had developed them into many widely divergent varieties. There were tropical varieties, and varieties which throve on the high plateau. These last were specially grown for slow freezing and grinding into a nourishing and easily preserved dehydrated starch powder.

The lowland people grew the sweet potato, a quite different plant. They cultivated a range of local fruits and vines which greatly enriched their dietary. It was in their country that the peppers grew, to add spice to the everyday stews and maize wafers.

Varieties of the pepper vine could also be chewed and spat into bowls of water with mashed starch to ferment into a drink with a fair amount of alcohol in it. Up in the highlands the same process, with maize as the basis, was used for brewing *chicha*. The Peruvians had no knowledge of such ferments as yeast. The chewing and spitting process, normally the work of the women, produced sufficient ptyalin to get fermentation going.

Drunkenness was a recurring passion among the Peruvian Indians. No festival was complete or satisfactory unless the majority of the community were incapable of either clear thought or action at the conclusion of the ceremonial events. But between the festivals the Indians behaved with a careful sobriety. Drunkenness at the wrong time was a hindrance to earning one's own living, and, worse still, to the production of the quota of goods for the benefit of the community. These surplus products formed the tributes to the Sun and the Inca. Therefore drunkenness was anti-social and not only frowned on by the villagers but punished by the authorities.

The most important drug in use in Peru was *coca*, the dried leaves of a shrub. This was commonly used to help one to endure hard toil over long periods. It was simply chewed, and sometimes lime seems to have been used with it. However it was usually carried as dried and crumbled leaves in little bags worn at the girdle. When working it minimized the little aches and pains and made one forget fatigue. When resting it induced a mild stupor and so helped to make the routine of everyday life more bearable. Naturally, it could be abused only too easily. But the tales of listless and filthy groups of

23

Storing potatoes

Addiction to *coca*

stupefied *coca* addicts belong to the period of the Spanish conquest and the sad times afterwards. In the first instance the Indians saw the whole of their social and economic order overthrown by strange conquerors from over the sea. Later on they found themselves without land or rights as citizens. Under foreign domination, however well intentioned, the people lost heart and found solace in gentle stupidity. They also achieved freedom from the more painful manifestations of hunger.

There was never a shortage of meat in Peru. A certain amount of hunting was permitted by the Inca on great festivals, in which the wild guanaco and deer might be captured, though little of the meat was distributed to the village communities. But the occasional slaughter of a llama for its leather and hair as well as the meat was quite proper for all villagers. They also kept cavies (guinea pigs), which they called *cui cui*, as a source of domesticated meat. The people of the coast hunted sea-lions, and of course enjoyed fishing with constant success. They faced no protein shortage.

At the ceremonial hunts game was driven into nets and usually pole-axed with metal-headed clubs. Fishing nets were made of cotton strings, hunting nets of cotton rope or leather thongs. The slings used by boys protecting the fields brought down birds for the family stew-pot. They were also used for driving game in the Royal Hunt ceremonies. The country was so well organized that really there was little need for hunting except as an ancient ceremonial custom. Similarly, with fishing no very elaborate techniques were used, for the reason that there was always abundance.

The herds of llamas kept on the highland plateau were mostly transport animals. When they were used as food the hides were prepared as leather, and the bones were used for tools and handles of implements. However, there were also herds of alpaca which were carefully watched over because they produced an excellent wool which was the staple material for clothing in the highland regions. The wild vicuña provided a much finer wool and this was collected as opportunity offered for spinning and weaving the delicate cloth from which the garments of the Inca nobility were made.

Alpaca wool was also used on the coast, but there the basic fibre was cotton which was cultivated in irrigated plantations.

As was usual in ancient Peru, a proportion of all llamas and alpacas were set aside for the Sun temples, and another proportion for the Inca. From these animals, especially from albinos, the special cloth dedicated for the garments of the highest social groups was woven. This highly specialized work was performed by the Maidens of the Sun, a group of selected young women who were partly of noble birth but who also included girls selected a little before puberty from among the general population. They were chosen because of considerable personal beauty, combined with gentle manners and graceful movement. They were taken from their families and kept as an enclosed order of nuns dedicated to the service of the Sun and his earthly representative, the Inca. The girls were dressed in white. In the convent they led an austere life in which the production of beautiful textile fabrics must have been one of the few pleasures. Some of these young ladies remained in dedicated virginity all their lives, becoming teachers and highly respected prophetesses. But many were selected by the Inca as gifts to visiting chiefs and noblemen. In these cases they left the convent and married. The marriages were as happy as a marriage by royal command might be, because a woman who had been a Maiden of the Sun was always greatly honoured by all around her.

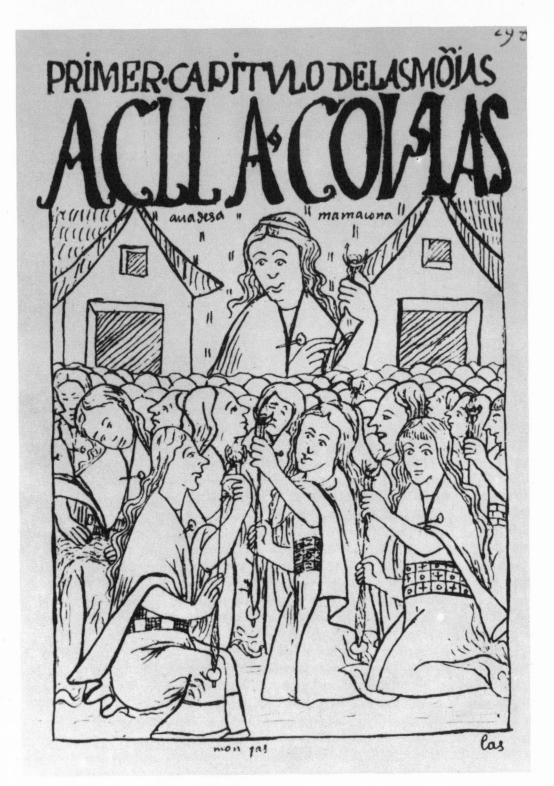

The Maidens of the Sun spinning thread

In the towns and villages all women could weave enough cloth for most of their family needs. As small girls they learned to spin and continued this activity all their lives. Every strand of cotton or alpaca was spun on a simple hand spindle. From this all the untold miles of thread used in Peru found their origin. The amount of work involved can be estimated by considering that even a coarse tunic made with twenty threads to the inch would take up a mile and a half (2½ kilometres) of thread. Weaving this would involve moving the heddle and throwing the shuttle of a simple back strap loom nearly four thousand times. A woman's long gown would take half as much work again. All this was needed for a simple weave, without taking any account of the beautiful tapestry weaves found on the better garments (plate 4).

Since lengths of cloth and made-up garments were burnt as offerings at the Sun festival, and thrown into rivers at the new year purification festivals, and as at least a third of the product of weaving was put aside in the Inca storehouses, the amount of textile made by the women of ancient Peru with their very primitive weaving and spinning apparatus is almost beyond calculation.

There is evidence of the existence of group workshops from times long before the Incas. In Inca times there can be no doubt that quite apart from the work of the Sun Maidens a good deal of fine cloth for festival use must have been made in communal factories. Whether these were organized as part of the public service or owned by district chiefs is not known. Neither do we know whether the weavers were detailed from their villages to spend a period in cloth production or whether they were a group of specialists recruited by proficiency and fed at the public expense. However, we can be sure that the arrangements were made locally because of the strict limitations placed upon regional costume and textile design by state regulation.

To judge by the woven patterns of existing textiles, the Peruvian women were mathematically minded and were capable of producing the most complicated geometrical patterns by counting stitches as they worked. They had no writing, but from a pre-Inca vase painting it is certain that they had pattern pieces beside them to use as guides when making tapestry. It was important that the design should not deviate from the local norm. Deviation was not so much a crime as a misfortune to be remedied by penitence and replacement of the offending material by a corrected version.

Dyeing was usually done in the yarn. The dyes were vegetable products in most cases, and from the specimens which have survived it is clear that the colours were light-resistant to a high degree and withstood age almost perfectly. A small amount of cloth was decorated by tie-dye techniques in the weft. Sometimes, after weaving, stamped and resist-dyeing were used, but they were not widely practised.

There was no fashion industry in Tahuantinsuyu. The basic style was common to all groups, but the decorations in embroidery, tapestry weaving, and headgear were all strictly regulated. No one was allowed to wear anything but the costume appropriate to the region where he was born, and of the quality determined by his rank (plate 3). In fact people felt that to masquerade in this way would be a sinful thing beneath contempt. From the point of view of the Inca oligarchy this was a valuable trait to be encouraged, because in any gathering one could immediately discover the home town of any person present. Thus it was easy to keep check on any separatist or conspiratorial tendencies.

The basic costume for women was a long gown, or long gown and tunic with a folded

Above. Weaving on a small loom from a late Chimu site

Below. The Sapa Inca with regional chiefs

CÕÇEJOREAL:DESTOS:REINOS
CAPACTGA·TAVANTIN
SVIO·CAMACHICOC·APOCONA

conzejo real destereyno

cloth head-dress, and a loose cloak. The waist was held in by a broad band of decorated cloth which gave a colourful contrast to the simple garments. At the neck a decorative pin with a big silver or bronze head was worn. Gold was worn only by girls of Inca descent. Flowers might be worn on festal occasions, but what flowers and how they were worn were strictly regulated by custom. Men wore a loincloth, and there is some evidence to suggest that some wore short breeches. They all wore tunics reaching a little above the knee, and all had broad waistbands. Fringes were worn just below the knee. Ear-rings were made for wearing in the pierced ear lobe, but really big ones were worn only by men of the Inca family, and of course were made of gold. Both sexes wore sandals of various patterns and some people used slippers plaited from straw.

Clothing was never tailored. Loom lengths sewn at the selvedges made up a tunic. But for some caps and belts cloth was woven on a loom which produced curved selvedges. There are examples of appliqué work, and cloth made up of pieces of complex shapes sewn together, but these are extremely rare. It is evident, however, that the straight lines of costume were due to taste, not technical ignorance.

The curious combination of high technical skill with the most primitive equipment is found in Peruvian ceramics just as in the textile manufactures. The Inca developed a kind of official pottery tradition which can be defined as a group of six standard forms made of fine clay and painted with geometric or near geometric patterns in red, black and white over a cream slip.

The clay was tempered with fine sand rather than potter's grog. It was mixed with great care to attain an even texture. Then it was coiled and modelled by hand. The Peruvians never invented the potter's wheel. The nearest they came was to use a large curved section of a broken pot to make a turntable in order to save themselves moving as they turned the coils of clay round and round to make the shape of the pot. By reducing the number of standard shapes the Inca-controlled peoples of the highlands greatly simplified the task of acquiring the skill needed to make accurate form and exact size in their vessels. Their painting was a geometric style ultimately derived from their ancestors in Tiahuanaco times, but so evolved that it is hardly recognizable. The simple beauty of exact geometry was varied a little to include standard symbols such as the Inca Flower, and lightning serpents. Judging by occasional burn marks on the cream slip on Inca period pots, the firing was in an open kiln, probably a pile of brushwood, or grass and llama-dung in regions where the country was more thoroughly deforested. The firing was always open, with a free flow of oxygen turning the paste of the vessels red. A temperature of about 950 degrees centigrade seems to have been kept up long enough for the pots to have oxidized right through, for it is rare indeed to find an Inca potsherd with the black core characteristic of hurried firing.

The coastal peoples of the Inca Empire, particularly the Chimu, had a quite different ceramic tradition. Even when they reproduced Inca forms, which, in spite of their simplicity, they managed to do without conviction, they used their own techniques of mould-made wares and frequent reduction firings. The moulds from which sections of composite pots were made consisted of thick clay cast over a model, which often seems to have been metal. The inner surfaces of the moulds are very smooth and accurately made, and they are all fired excellently to a hard reddish biscuit quality. Some of the vases were made by pressing sheets of soft clay into the moulds and then trimming the edges

Above. Inca pottery from Peru (left) and Ecuador

Below. Chimu (left) and Cara figure vases of the Inca period, showing variations in style minimized by a common imitation of metal-working techniques

31

with a bronze knife. Where relief was high some potters added a little extra clay to the places where pressure might split the sheet of clay. But in a number of cases we find evidence that the moulds were filled with a thick slurry of clay which was rocked over the mould until it dried and set. This process sometimes left areas of clay which were eggshell-thin, and which have broken after firing. In either method the clay shrunk as it dried, and so when it was leather-hard it fell easily out of the mould. The cast sections of the pot were luted together with wet clay used like a glue on the joint, and then the whole vessel was dried slowly and carefully. On the coast firing was sometimes conducted in free air and then the pots burned red, but it was the fashion among the Chimu to make black pottery. No kilns have been found from which to check the exact method, but it is safe to say that the pots were fired either inside a larger pot or in a hole in the ground stuffed with smouldering chopped grass, wood chips and so on. The air was excluded as far as possible, perhaps by putting leaves or seaweed over the top of the "stove". This process raised the pit to the necessary temperature in excess of 900 degrees centigrade, but with oxygen excluded the firing took place in an atmosphere of carbon dioxide and the pot turned dark grey all through. When a pot subjected to this reduced firing process was cool it remained a hard dark-grey colour. Some of the coarser pots were burnished and polished a shiny black, but the best ones were left a dark iron-grey colour. When they were filled with water they looked rather like tarnished silver, which was presumably the potters' intention since silver was the material for the tableware of many wealthy inhabitants of the Chimu kingdom, even in the period of Inca rule.

It is certain that in the highlands women were potters, but one is not so sure for the coastal region, where certainly in earlier times men modelled the remarkable portrait vases of the Mochica culture. But although women worked on the high-temperature technology of pottery, men were the metallurgists. There was probably a very good reason in the fact that a pot could be made near the home with the children playing around, but metalworking involved journeying to the sources of ore.

The gold, which belonged to the Inca, seems to have all been placer-mined. There is no evidence of the driving of galleries to follow veins of auriferous stones. The gold was made into ornaments of many kinds; necklaces, bracelets, ear-discs, and small images of deities. However, works of hardly imaginable magnificence were made, like the great golden sheet on the end wall of Ccoricancha which showed the Sun and Moon among the stars and the outline of the history of creation. A century and a half after the conquerors had melted down the gold, Indian families remembered this wonder and Salcamayhua recorded its general design in his book about the Inca times. The Spaniards only recorded the great golden cornice which ran round the outside of the whole building of Ccoricancha, gold without any disgrace of ornament, like a ray of the Sun itself. This to the Incas was a holy thing, not wealth nor coin, but divine beauty.

One of the wonders of the Inca palace in Cuzco was a garden in which maize plants were made of silver with the beautiful leaves in rippling sheet metal all set with the cobs in pure gold. It expressed a love for the maize plant as a holy thing and a source of life worthy of the Sun and Moon. Again we come to an understanding that the quality of preciousness attributed to these metals was something quite different in Peru from what it is in the civilized world of today.

Silver was mined from ore, and since it is found in association with copper and often

Chimu black-ware vase

with such metals as tin and antimony we have the foundations of local metallurgical industries.

The smiths understood very well by immediate inspection what could be obtained from the ores. They used bronze wedges and stone hammers for breaking up the minerals. The smelting was a surprisingly small-scale process. It was entirely conducted in open-work clay bowls which were packed with burning charcoal around a fire-clay crucible. There were no bellows in Inca Peru, but forced draught was obtained by groups of metallurgical assistants who sat around the little furnaces blowing through copper tubes to keep up the temperature. To aid their work the forces of nature were enlisted, so the furnaces were assembled on windy hillsides where the natural draught would help the lung-power of the assistants. The metallurgist selected the ores to be melted, and, when making bronze, mixed his ores by measure. The idea of weighing out exact quantities was never perfected except among a few people on the coastal regions. The crucible was heated up and as the ore melted into a magma some method of skimming it, perhaps by stirring with a metal rod, was resorted to. Eventually the crucible of metal was lifted with tongs made of a green withy, and the contents were poured into an open mould which had been pre-heated so that it would not explode.

One reads of hillsides in the mountains illuminated by hundreds of these small furnaces used by a tribal group of metallurgists. This is not surprising when one considers the great number of silver vases found in the coastal region, and the generally widespread use of bronze for tools and weapons. The quantity of metal used was quite considerable, though one metallurgist and his team of assistants could probably not produce much more than 500 lb (230 Kg.) of bronze in a year. It is quite probable that the long-continued use of charcoal for smelting by this method accounted for the greater part of the deforestation of the Andes. Metallurgy was well developed a thousand years before the time of the Incas, and the rate of production was high from the beginning.

As an example of almost incredible skill we may mention that copper objects were sometimes welded in ancient Peru. Metallurgical studies have proved this without revealing the technique, but it was probably dependent on the use of a blowpipe on small exposed areas of an object otherwise tightly packed in charcoal. Another remarkable skill was exhibited by the silversmiths and goldsmiths who could beat out of a solid block of metal a beaker some eight inches deep and three inches in diameter without breaking it (plate 6).

Metals were sometimes decorated by diestamping, but more often a repoussé technique was used which consisted of gently beating the metal over dies made from stone. The whole art of *cire-perdue* casting was well understood, and the most complex forms were cast by this technique in both gold and bronze. They included an abundance of little bells which were used as jangles on both necklaces and pendants as well as on the fringes of garments.

Bronze, because of its composition by the handful of ore rather than the ounce, varied immensely in metal content, but it was generally of good quality. The edge of bronze tools was hardened by first heating it and then beating rapidly as the metal cooled. It must not be taken to the point where the cooled metal heated again by reason of the beating. Use gradually softened the edge and then blunted it, but it could be easily restored to hardness by warming and beating it down to the point of coldness. Bronze tools included heavy axes, spiked club-heads, chisels, digging-stick points, hammers, pins, needles, and the curved tumi knife. It was an alloy for practical use much more than for ornament. Its use established the Peruvians as the most advanced technologists of all the native peoples of the American continent.

The bronze chisels and drills were employed very successfully in working wood (plate 17). Boxes were made jointed together and covered with low-relief carving, almost like textile design. Wooden figures were carved with the solidity and massive proportions beloved of Peruvian artists. They were not seeking realism, but a formal expression of simple power. Delicacy was often achieved in small objects such as a carved head of a doll, or a small balance beam from the coast. There was a good deal of wooden furniture of which nothing remains, but it included quite ambitious works such as the carrying chair for the Inca. Tool handles and digging-sticks were made simply for strength rather than elegance.

For domestic use there were elegant wooden goblets known as *kero* (plate 7), as well as wooden bowls and dishes which were simple in form and almost perfect in proportion. Many of them were inlaid and painted with colour. In some cases mastic gum mixed with powder colours was used; and it has recently been announced that some of the

34

Plate 4. The Inca Sun God in kelim weave, and a woman's workbasket showing her raw brown and white cotton, bronze embroidery needles, and spools of dyed thread ready for tapestry weaving. From the Peruvian coast in the Inca period *British Museum. Photo: Derrick E. Wi*

Above. Chimu repoussé silverware of the Inca period   *Below*. Bronze bells, *cire-perdue* casting

ate 5. Necklace with beads of gold, turquoise, copper carbonate, rock crystal
d carnelian. From a grave in the Chimu region. The beads are polished but retain
e original form of the pebbles from which they were made. *Miss Kemper Collection*.
hoto: *Derrick E. Witty*

coloured paint was a variant of true lacquer, though this was never developed to Chinese standards.

Navigation employed a good deal of wood, not only canes, reed, and great logs of balsa wood, but also hard water-resistant timbers carved into magnificently designed centre-boards and steering paddles. The rhythmic designs on these works remind one of the tapestries of the central coast peoples.

Wood played a useful part in weapons, forming the stems of the typical Inca "halberd" and the strong staves used for bronze-headed maces. Especially chosen stems of wood were used for making throwing-sticks, and in some parts of the country for making powerful bows. Wood was not greatly used for building. Light constructions supported brushwood for thatched roofs, but as far as possible natural branches were used for this purpose because of the chronic shortage of timber.

One must not forget that for cutting timber and squaring wooden posts the stone axe was often superior to a bronze one because of its more dependable cutting edge. The blade was set into a socket in the axe handle, and was rarely very large. But apart from axe blades, chisels, and scrapers for smoothing flat surfaces, stone was not greatly used for tools. Peru was in a late phase of the Bronze Age where stone was only retained for a limited number of special purposes as far as tools and weapons were concerned.

However, the Peruvians in Inca times, particularly the highland peoples, were among the greatest stone-workers in all history. They worked hard stone for jewellery (plate 5), using rock crystal, carnelian, and hard blue and green stones similar to jade and turquoise. In many cases they simply polished a beautiful natural stone and inlaid it in gold. Even where cutting had been extensive, the surface was carefully finished to give the effect of supreme smoothness rather than simply a high gloss. Stone vessels were made for ceremonial use, and the forms have a simple abstract cubic quality which is unmistakable (plate 11).

There can be no doubt that there was an Inca aesthetic which determined proportion and mass with as much care as classical Europeans used the idea of the "golden mean". All parts of a stone object were related to each other in size and quality. The result is not one of airy delicacy or superb balance, but of a statement of fact made without any qualifying factors. It was this feeling for formal mass in stone which made it easy for the Inca shrines to include many sacred objects, called *huacas*, which vary from great natural rock masses such as the Kenko Stone (plate 16) near Cuzco to simple natural *objets trouvés* which they felt must have significance because of their intrinsic quality. The feeling of significance was translated by the Peruvians very naturally into an emotion of religious awe.

State building was a matter for architects who thought in terms of aesthetics as well as of utility. There were even relief maps made for blocks of construction and whole quarters of towns. In the great days of the Incas, public building was no haphazard erection of great walls, but a carefully designed aesthetic construction. It may seem very strange to the European eye, but it has a strength and simplicity which expresses the quality of stone as well as the greatness of purpose of the Inca family.

The greatest amount of building in Inca Peru comprised, of course, the simple huts of the villagers. On the coasts they built walls of sun-dried clay known to us as adobe. Roofs were of little use, a thin scatter of reeds on brushwood, or, better still, a cloth awning,

Carving from balsa centre-board

were perfect protection on the hot, rainless coastal plain. Up in the mountains the rectangular huts were made of stone dry-walling surmounted by a light wooden frame-work supporting a very thick grass thatch. This was protection against wind and storm as well as a good heat insulation.

Villages were built by the joint labour of all the people living there. If a young couple married, their neighbours built the house for them. Their work, and their future children, all added to the possibilities of fuller life for the community as a whole. But each village was usually in a tributary relationship to a town. The town must contain storehouses, buildings for the civil service, army quarters, a governor's residence, and above all a Sun temple. The growth of construction from village to town was simple and natural. But specialists were needed for the erection of large public buildings.

In the coastal towns of the Chimu country, adobe was an all-sufficient building material. It could be moulded as required, decorated by simple carving and lime wash, and held together by simply softening the joints with water and so sticking them together. Often walls such as those of the Chimu capital, Chan Chan, and the great temple pyramid at Pachacamac were elaborately sculptured and painted in vivid colours. A little topping of thatch was all that was needed to protect them from an occasional rainstorm, an event which might occur once or twice in a lifetime.

Wall of a palace at Cuzco

In the highlands, palaces, temples and fortresses were built of massive blocks of stone without mortar. The stones were polished and beaten into shape by stone balls repeatedly dropped on them. It was important for the joints between stones to fit accurately because no mortar was used (plates 2, 14). It was important for the balance of weights to be accurate so that when the frequent earthquakes jolted the buildings the stones as a whole would jump up and then fall back into place without any danger of collapsing. Many of the great fortresses were built of truly gigantic stones. These included some fortified houses in Cuzco itself. But many of the palaces were built of smaller but solid stones laid in neat courses of masonry. Courtyards were arranged with a sense of beauty, and round towers for storage were a feature of the construction within the courtyard which was enclosed by the walls of rooms around.

The buildings of an Inca city were sombre without, but rich hangings spread brilliance within, and some of the openings were framed by painted wooden doorposts. It was a typically Peruvian mixture of sombre grandeur with a brilliant sense of fantasy in minor decoration.

The construction of a city was the height of the arts in ancient Peru. It was an expression of the social organization of the state. Here lay all the links of government, the record offices, the messenger services, the army barracks and fortress, the storehouses of the Inca and the sacred shrine where the Sun was worshipped as lord over all the other *huacas* and spirit powers. Always people were moving about on their business within a city. Here the great festivals found a fit place for mass celebrations. Here passed trade and news. It was all made as efficient as possible, and it was expressed in a unique kind of architecture. The culmination was, of course, in Cuzco, the navel of the universe and the seat of the Sun's earthly descendant, the Sapa Inca, and of his High Priest who assisted him in the magical worship in Ccoricancha.

40

Chapter Two

THE ADMINISTRATION OF THE INCAS

From the last chapter it will have become clear that the peoples of the Inca empire were involved in a mesh of government which penetrated right down into family organization. The diffusion of power was a matter of religion because it derived ultimately from Inti, the Sun God. Therefore the Sapa Inca, being the closest in descent from the great Father in the sky, was the source of all earthly power. In this his position was strikingly similar to that of the Pharaoh in ancient Egypt.

The Sapa Inca Huayna Ccapac

There was no question of the Inca being bound by the same regulations as his people. His position demanded that, like the Sun, he should be amenable only to the compulsion of the passage of the seasons. In this pilgrimage through time he led the people. He turned the first sod at the ploughing festival, he led the offerings at the harvest, and he was alone in Ccoricancha when the sun struck the golden wall at the Sun Festival.

The Sapa Inca was in fact the State, for he was a magical sun king of the type that Louis XIV would have wished to emulate. The Sapa Inca as the Sun Lord was responsible for the growth and fertility of his land. His touch was a blessing, but if one was not worthy his glance might destroy. Whenever he passed, people bowed their heads to the ground, for it was not fitting that ordinary humans should look on his countenance. His only communion was with the members of the Inca family, the descendants of previous Incas, all of whom had inherited to some degree the quality of holiness. The greatest of human blessings was the possibility that the Sapa Inca should take a woman to his bed. Thereby she was glorified and her children became members of the Inca clan. Thus, in an officially monogamous state, the Inca himself was the head of a polygamous family breeding future rulers and administrators. In the generations immediately preceding the time of Topa Inca Yupanqui, the custom had been established that the Sapa Inca must be the offspring of the ruling Inca and his eldest sister. Thus the divine life was perpetuated on earth. One notes that in chronicles of native origin the name of the Ccoya, or Empress, is given with the name of each Inca.

Stone bowl showing the Inca and his Ccoya

The numbers of the Inca family were continually expanding. They were fully employed as military commanders, heads of state institutions, and the executive and administrative grades of the enormous civil service. Inca princesses of various lines of descent from the previous Sapa Incas were employed in the normal women's duties of weaving and embroidery within their families, though many became Maidens of the Sun, and some were given great diplomatic powers when they were married to conquered local chiefs, so that their children should bring Inca family powers to rule their future subjects.

The political situation of Inca Peru is quite beyond definition in Western political terms. It was a complete dictatorship of one man; it was administration by an oligarchy; it was a situation of state-controlled public welfare; it was a situation where every individual had responsibility to the state and received benefits from the state. It cannot be used as a modern argument for or against either fascism, communism, monarchy or democracy. It had within itself seeds of all those possibilities, but it was unique in its period in the world, perhaps in the whole of human history, although the Egyptians had formulated some such concept of government in the great days of the Old Kingdom three thousand years earlier in time and half way round the earth from Peru.

The incorporation of the subject tribes into the Inca hierarchy through the marriages with their ruling families was an expedient which the Incas found necessary once they had extended their power beyond the Cuzco valley. The wars with the Chanca confederacy taught them that divine right was not enough, but that the inspiration from the Sun was to be expressed in statesmanship as well as simple military power. They had not only to defeat opposition but to incorporate the conquered tribes in such a way that they benefited from the change.

When the local Curaca became a relative by marriage of the divine Sapa Inca he felt that he acquired something more than his previous chieftainship. Insofar as his people gained by the greater prosperity which came from incorporation in the large-scale production and storage enterprises of the Inca, his local prestige similarly advanced. Because of this policy many independent tribes sent messengers to Cuzco to seek admission to Tahuantinsuyu. They were then given favours which were even better than those awarded to tribes who submitted after battle. Their provinces were sooner honoured by a visit from the Sapa Inca, and the nobles were allowed to wear clothes of special honour to denote their favoured official position. The marriages of the chiefs to the Inca princesses were more brilliant. But the treatment of their children was no different, for no honour could be greater than to be born of divine Inca family. All these local princelings were taken for education in Cuzco so that they should grow up to honour their kinsman the Sun and to be proud to wear the specially woven belts and ear-rings which marked them as having Inca lineage.

The education of an Inca prince was very sound. He was given an apartment in a stone palace in Cuzco, and he was issued with the standard quantities of food and clothing of the quality suitable to his social rank. Servants were provided, too, so that he could be judged quietly by his treatment of those under his command. If he came from the outer provinces everything was done to make him feel that the Inca way of life was the perfect one and that he should teach his father's people to follow his mother's customs. His first lessons were in keeping accounts. That was very important. A chief had to under-

The Sapa Inca inspecting stores and *quipu*

stand how many people he ruled, how many houses they occupied, how much grain they produced, how many llamas were in the pastures, how many people were available for labour gangs, how many young men were to be sent to the army, and how many marriages were to be arranged each year. All this was recorded on knotted cords of many colours. The colours told the subject of the *quipu*, as it was called, and the knots counted numbers in a decimal system. Later in life a chief might not have to use a *quipu*, but it was better if he could personally check the records kept by his Quipucamayoc or Accountant. The *quipus* were also used for scientific work, since some of them contain numbers which record the rhythms of the moon and planets among the stars. This was of course important for chiefs to know, since it was believed that the positions of the planets and the state of the moon influenced almost everything that took place on earth. They also marked the seasons, and it was always important for a chief to know which day was the right one on which to call his people to celebrate the festivals.

The students had to learn a good deal of simple astronomy, because the Incas celebrated their great feasts on the days when the sun was highest and lowest in the sky, but the people had festivals connected with the position of the moon. It was always difficult to adjust the two calendars, since the moon month of twenty-nine and a half days does not fit the solar year of three hundred and sixty-five and a quarter days.

History was taught by means of painted boards which had pictures on them showing great events. The stories associated with them were remembered because they were preserved in rhythmic verses which are easy to keep in the mind. There were, of course, specialist historians in the court of every chief, but those who were responsible for administration should be well acquainted with local traditions.

44

Above. Section of a *quipu* *Below*. Sun festival

For princes of tribes with customs different from those of the Incas there were courses on administration and social custom. The Inca rule depended on the acceptance of uniformity in religion as well as in social usage. Although the provincials were allowed to worship their own gods, there was always a place for the Sun at the head of the local hierarchy of heaven. Everywhere the Inca princes, cousins and second cousins of the Inca, were proud of their relationship with the divine father Inti, the Sun. Everywhere they introduced his worship among their people, because their own authority came to depend upon it. The indoctrination courses at Cuzco were of vital political consequence to the Inca empire, and brought much peace of mind to all local rulers who accepted them.

There was no narrowness in education for the young Incas. They were made to mix with intelligent young citizens who were not Incas but who had been selected for the state service. And for all young people there was a good deal of organized physical training. The exercises were largely warlike. In these the boys of the unimportant families had some advantage since they early acquired skill with sling and club in driving away pests from the fields, defending the llama herds from foxes and birds of prey, and, of course, herding the stubborn llamas. Sometimes youngsters of all social groups became involved in pitched battles when one *ayllu* or tribal division quarrelled with another. The *ayllus* were in many ways like clans, but with place of residence counted as well as family. With the Incas it was different. Their *ayllu* system was entirely based on descent from particular Sapa Incas of past reigns. The *ayllu* system was very important, since it made for local unities, and for a spirit of competition between rival *ayllus* which kept the level of social production high. The Inca *ayllus* were, more than anything else, a means of identifying the relative rank of individuals in the immense family hierarchy. But in youth membership of an *ayllu* was an incentive to competitive struggle. Group contested with group for honours.

For the youths in the schools in Cuzco there was an annual competition. Boys of about fourteen were taken by their instructors, given a simple coarse tunic and a waistband, but neither sandals nor weapons. They were mixed in groups of which the members did not usually know each other and then selected as teams, each of nine boys, who were taken to different points around Cuzco and then turned loose to fend for themselves for nine days. This amounted to a survival course. The cold on the mountains and the dangers from wild beasts such as puma and wild dog meant that the boys must plan to make slings from plaited grass and clubs or spears from any stems of bushes which they could cut down with roughly chipped stone choppers. They had to find places where they could nest in grass sheltered from the winds, and know how to make a fire. They must also be good at hunting edible animals and able to cook them. On the last day the teams had to approach the exercise grounds at Ccolcampata without being seen until they could burst on to the ground and line up for a foot race. In this they all raced towards a stone goal near which the Sapa Inca was enthroned. The winner of the race was given a small prize by the Sapa Inca, and was treated with great honour. His glory was reflected on all the members of his *ayllu*.

The conditions of the race were strictly fair, and any accusation against the judges of the exercises, which preceded the races, was investigated with great care. Any unjust judge would be killed for such a crime. The fairness of it all can be gauged by the fact that the only Inca heir-apparent who ever won the competition was Prince Tupac, who later became the great Sapa Inca, Topa Inca Yupanqui. His later wisdom and energy bore out the early promise of his remarkable boyhood victory in the games.

The Inca families were fitted into the national organization in many ways, but they were not given a monopoly except in the highest offices of state. The Inca through his local administration watched the population for the appearance of talented young people who could be brought into the public service. Not only were beautiful and clever girls chosen for the Maidens of the Sun, but boys were also selected for the recording and planning branches of government service. These youngsters were honoured according to their ability and found a special reward in the greater freedom which state service gave them compared to the cosy, restriction-protected life of the usual small farmer. By this arrangement the Sapa Inca bound the populace to him quite independently of the family ties of the Inca clan.

The basic social unit within the state was the family of three generations. Children, parents, and the old folk were united by common work in food production, house building and clothes making. Usually their dwellings were built close to each other and their allotted field strips were near by so that they could all work to help each other. The head of the household was the married man. He was accountable to the head of ten families for the account of crops and weaving, and for the supply of family help in any communal enterprise such as harvesting, planting, building of new field strips, and so on. He it was who attended the distribution of materials from the imperial storehouses in time of necessity. The children all received a minimum allowance of food and clothing, which was made up from local reserves if family production was insufficient for unavoidable reasons. In any case, a newly married couple were excused taxes of their produce for a year, in order to allow them time to set up house and prepare for the children to arrive. Grandparents were assessed at low rates of tax to compensate for their loss of strength after long service to the community.

The village head of ten families had to keep simple records for the head of fifty families, and he in turn would account to the head of a hundred families. This was the highest rank in the usual village or small town hierarchy. These officials kept records very exactly on the knotted string *quipus* which they took at least once a year to deposit with the Quipucamayoc at the nearest town government office. They were very careful with these records, because the amount of all allowances to the village and of all tribute payable to the state depended on their preservation.

There were family group leaders of higher numerical units, but one is not sure if they performed any very practical function as far as their "constituents" were concerned. They seem to have been recording officers whose statistics became important when large movements of labour or supplies were necessary. They could have had only a rather general local patriotism. However, one gains the impression that the lower units were very closely related to the people and looked after communal interests quite as well as those of the state. It is probable that the statistics were somewhat adjusted so as to keep the taxation within bearable limits. This would have been connived at by the higher officials because the Inca rulers hated oppression for the very good reason that it bred discontent. However, it is quite clear that the pressure of public opinion was usually in favour of paying the taxes to the Inca and the Sun. It was well understood that they were returned to the people in the form of good government and efficient protection, and they were always a government reserve for use in times of famine. Opposition to paying taxes because of selfish considerations was hardly considered a possibility in Peru. Adjustments for the welfare of a village were quite a different thing. It may be that this showed a weakness of self-realization among the people, but it certainly made life easier in a hard country.

The officials of a town or province were an efficient civil service, under control from higher units of government and, finally, from the Sapa Inca himself. Any falsification of accounts or exploitation for personal gain was sharply punished. This applied to all crimes against the individual or state property. The rank of the offender was not a mitigating circumstance, in fact it only made punishment more painful. There were no prisons, and punishment might be death, but more often was a public mutilation such as ear-cropping, cutting off the nose or lopping hands or feet. The unfortunate victim was given good medical treatment, and then supplied with the standard allowance of food and clothing. But he was never allowed concealment, so that whoever passed through the district might see the vivid living evidence of the penalty for crime.

Sometimes the Inca officials feared local insurrection in favour of old tribal usages. If their suspicions proved well founded, whole populations might be moved. The action was made as merciful as possible, and the *mitimaes,* as such forced settlers were called, were given tax relief while settling the new lands.

There was no change in the general social condition of *mitimaes.* They preserved their old village allegiances, and shared fields in the same way. In many cases they were involved in an exchange of small sections of the population in which each transported group took over the houses and fields of the other. They still retained their old costume and the distinctive ornaments and head-dresses. Although this was a very welcome way of making people feel at home in new surroundings, it had a real purpose of keeping them distinct among their new neighbours, so that the local governors could see that they were not mixing dangerously or trying to form an alliance to oppose the administration. The rule followed was always to move populations to a similar terrain to that of their homeland. Lowland people were transported to other lowland areas, people of the mountains found new mountains were allocated to them. It was a matter of production policy, since the highlanders would not have been able to live or work efficiently in the heavy hot air of the lower regions of the country. The lowlanders would suffer also if they came to the thin air and bitter cold of the plateau three miles or more above sea level.

The Inca efficiency in combating the climate extended to the messengers who travelled on the Sapa Inca's business along the great road system. Teams of these runners, or Chasquis, were stationed at posting houses at distances which varied between a furlong and three miles according to the terrain. No runner ever left his own area. The lowland men ran from their home station on the road to the next post station where they passed on their message or load to the local team and then waited for a return load. Special teams were kept for the short but ardous journeys of the mountain ascents. Others worked only on the roads and bridges of the highlands. The system was so efficient that fish packed in seaweed could be taken 250 miles from the coast up to the city of Cuzco and arrive fresh and sweet for the royal dinner.

A Chasqui carrying messages

Usually the messengers carried information, normally accompanied by a bundle of knotted cord *quipus*. As the runners approached their next post they called out, and the next team of runners came out. They received the *quipus* and a short verbal message to go with them and so passed on news and information. None of them ever learned more than a simple phrase or two which were transmitted by word of mouth and were necessary for the interpretation of the *quipus* by those who understood the system.

The interchange of all government information took place through the messenger service. Each town was a node in a network of roads and trackways covering the whole country. Basically there were three north-south highways with crossroads at all traversable valleys. The information transmitted by messengers was mainly for area administration at lower than provincial level, but each provincial capital had its own record offices where information was collated by the quipucamayocs. The knotted records were, in effect, an information file classified under different headings by the colour and design of the main cord to which others were attached. The translation was verbal, and the basic information was available through the trained memory of specialist record keepers and advisers. The information was considered and translated into action by the officials of the highest administrative grades available. Eventually a precis of all information from the whole of Tahuantinsuyu was available for the Sapa Inca if he wished to consider any particular problem.

The nature of the state organization meant that the Sapa Inca was a restless man. On the great festivals he was normally at Cuzco, but he was often engaged in a slow-moving royal progress through the provinces of Tahuantinsuyu. It was considered improper to hurry the great one, and twenty miles a day was regarded as a long journey. This was probably very true when one considers that the progress was made in a litter borne on the shoulders of two dozen noblemen. When the Inca moved in such a progress, the train of people was enormous. The officers and servants of the court were all concerned, and detachments of the army as well as hundreds of servants of various degrees were necessary companions of the divine king. It was of course important that every point of the journey should be planned well in advance, not only for arranging the commissariat, but also for securing the supply of regular information, which was done by a constant re-routing of messages as the position of the court changed. The organization was most impressive, and seems to have worked with great efficiency because it was conceived as a simple operation necessary for the welfare of the provinces and for the expansion of the benevolent divine power of the Sapa Inca.

By no means all of the governmental system was Inca in origin. Even in their highland capital they inherited a tradition of social regulation at tribal level. This was ultimately derived from the ancient city of Tiahuanaco, which was also ruled by a sun-worshipping oligarchy, to judge by the figure of the weeping sun god on the monolithic gateway. The symbols on the figure equate it very closely indeed with the Inca concept of their god, Inti. The idea of roads was also present in pre-Inca times both beside the coast and along the mountains linking areas on the eastern slopes of the Andes. The coastal roads and cities were the older in their origins, and the social system of the coastal kingdoms, particularly that of the Chimu, was as fully planned as that of the Inca. With the fall of the great fortress of Paramonga, the Inca took over the Chimu kingdom as a complete organizational unit. The communications system was similar, the *quipu* was

The Sapa Inca and Ccoya travelling

the method of transmitting information, the division of the people into kinship groups was similar to that of the *ayllu* of the highland people.

When one considers all the evidence it becomes clear that the Incas developed local traditional custom and built it up as a unifying scheme which could work effectively among any people, either with a similar background or to whom the idea of a planned economy was something new. This does not at all detract from the reputation of the great Sapa Incas; they remain among the really successful political organizers of history. They are of a quality of mind which can only be compared with T'ai Tsung, the first emperor and organizer of T'ang China, or with Lenin in our own age. To adapt the old, to build on it and induce organic growth in order to make something new on such a scale is an achievement which is stupendous, and in Peru it has a special quality since it developed in conjunction with a basic economy of early Bronze Age type.

Such great advances in a short space of time demand a certain sweep of vision which does not take much account of individuals. The Incas had an initial advantage in the fatalistic temperament of the American Indians. There was a willingness to accept life within a series of restrictions, and an ability to express the highest flights of individuality in communal activity. The great festivals were an organized operatic spectacle in which everyone took part as a performer. The great communal labour activities all commenced with a joyful ceremony with everybody in gala dress. The Peruvians did not keep their people happy with *panem et circenses*. The growing of the corn for bread was in itself the joyous communal festival. Work was a kind of creative satisfaction, and when it grew very heavy on the heart there were always the peace-bringing *coca* leaves to chew to sink one gently down to the level of the common unconscious.

The fermented *chicha* was also much in evidence, but it seems that in Inca times the dances at the festivals were performed before the allowances of *chicha* reduced everybody to a golden haze of stupor. Plays were performed, but the traces which remain show that they were pleasant romances and moral interludes. They were traditional, but probably less important in building social unity than the folk-tales and songs, which even today still echo the haunting beauty and sadness of the passing of life and summer among the mountains and along the desert coasts of Tahuantinsuyu. One can never know if the Inca dynasty exploited this quality of sober enjoyment of life among their subjects. The probability is that it was shared by the Inca family themselves and was thought to be the normal way of humanity. Indeed, the Inca social system did not take much account of the individual person, yet the individual must have found a good deal of happiness in the feeling of belonging within the community.

The acceptance of life's hardships begins for all people when they find themselves obliged to accept the rules of the family circle. In Peru the life of children was as happy as with most peoples. The youngsters played and worked all in one, taking a child's part in all family activities and learning gradually. The presence of social order was felt to be natural from the days of the earliest experiences of helping the family to grow a surplus of crops to become tribute for the Sun and the Inca.

Later the contact became still closer, for the young men who had not been selected for some special training — that is, the great majority of them — were selected for army service.

There was no avoidance of service. It was part of the natural order, and though the

Corn-planting festival at Cuzco

idea behind the creation of Tahuantinsuyu was the spreading of universal peace, it was understood by all that often it would be necessary to use force and sacrifice one's life in the service of the divine Sapa Inca. The Inca armies were in part a public service organization, bringing materials and food from one part of the country to another as they might be needed, and providing trained personnel for essential construction work on defences and transport. In war they were sometimes defending Tahuantinsuyu from barbarian invaders, mostly wild tribes from the Amazon forests who were seeking no more than occasional plunder from their rich neighbours. At other times the empire was expanding and then very serious campaigns were planned.

The army was a selective service body. Training began innocently enough through physical culture courses in wrestling, weight lifting, sling shooting and so on when boys were about ten years old. The village elders, or the teachers where there were regular schools, reported on the boys. After they had been working in the communal fields for some time they were again recorded so that when a request for a draft came from the army command it was immediately known which young men were suited to become warriors, and which should be taken only as carriers and craftsmen. The plan was never to remove the whole of the young men of a district, but to keep the numbers changing through short term service drafting. The periods of service varied according to climatic conditions. Not all young men returned to the normal civilian life; those among them who showed the qualities of discipline and bravery needed in a warrior who fought his opponents hand-to-hand, were likely to be ordered to remain permanently with the army.

The army was arranged on a decimal system very like the Roman organization of decurions and centurions leading men from the ranks. The Peruvians added higher commanders of a thousand, five thousand and ten thousand men. The usual procedure was for these officers to be selected from the ranks on their record of performance in the lower grades. Army commanders were directly under the control of the Sapa Inca. The storehouses of the Inca were primarily for the use of the army as it moved from place to place.

At the levels where military and civil administration merged there was a valuable area of social integration. The army kept garrisons in fortresses and detachments at storehouses, and so were ever-ready guardians of public peace. They also provided, through their control of the storehouses, a guarantee that if local crops failed there would at least be some simple food and clothing for the local people. But perhaps even more important in popular esteem was the fact that the storehouses enabled the army to feed and clothe itself, thus preventing robbery of the kind which went on in medieval Europe whenever an army passed through the countryside.

The Peruvian army system was not well adapted for the promotion of individual glory. Its purpose was to defend and extend Tahuantinsuyu and its sanction was theocratic, from Inti the Sun God, Father of the Sapa Inca. When this tradition was broken, on the occasion when the usurper Atahuallpa used a northern army to destroy the army of his brother, the true Sapa Inca, the shock was so great that the whole state suffered a kind of paralysis in the face of the Spanish invasion.

Forced labour was mostly called for on a selective plan, much like army recruitment. When some natural calamity, such as an earthquake, had caused disaster beyond local

54

capacity to repair, reserves of labour were mobilized and moved in to help reconstruct roads, rebuild retaining walls for the fields, and generally clear away difficulties until the point was reached where the local population could once more fend for itself. After such an event taxes were remitted for a year, until a new harvest had filled the local granaries before the state took its share. Sometimes it was necessary to erect great public works, and then reserves of stonemasons and labourers were called into action. They could be mobilized to erect palaces and fortresses at surprising speed, because a sufficient number of people with the needed skills could be brought together quickly. Stone-cutters and architectural masons were put to work as teams. Erection gangs toiled under specialist builders to pile up walls. The woodworkers were put to work erecting roof beams. All was organized so that even with primitive, and time-consuming, techniques the time-and-motion study required was so accurate that there was no waste of man-power. When the day for erection came, the stones were finished and the teams were ready to drag them and pile them in place. Then the woodworkers were ready to per-form their part of the task. The necessary access to the road system was completed at the same time so that as soon as construction was complete the furnishing required could be moved in from the official storehouses.

Local labour forces were called together by the headmen under instruction from the district governors to keep the many roads in repair. Each of the fantastic suspension bridges which spanned the Andean gorges was cared for by the local community, and regularly inspected by local overseers so that replacements of the osier cables or wooden floorboards could be made at the first sign of decay. If an accident occurred it was re-ported to the local governor, and the responsible members of the community supposed to be in charge of upkeep of roads would be summarily punished. The Inca govern-ment realized very well how vital good communications were to their system.

Amid all this organized life there was little room for individual affairs. No doubt people were proud of their grain production or weaving as individual craftsmen, and families might be proud of the way in which they kept house and cared for their furnish-ings. But even the basic family was not a totally free institution.

Marriage was a compulsory activity except for the Maidens of the Sun and a few people thought to be inspired by the spirits and outside human nature. The selection of bride and groom was made by the headmen who decided on the correct pairs by their age and place of residence. It was preferred that the young couple should belong to a closely circumscribed neighbourhood, and in fact it was most unusual for anyone to express a desire to marry into a community which wore different distinguishing marks in the head-dress. It was not thought proper to marry strangers. Since marriage was prescribed by custom and social considerations demanded marriage at the age of maturity when the man was twenty-five and the woman eighteen, they must be in similar physical con-dition and of comparable social status. When one takes into consideration the question of kinship affinities it is clear that there was no real choice about whom one should marry. It was simply a fact that for the mass of the people one husband and one wife lived their lives as an economic partnership, and they probably knew all about what it would be like long before the day of the marriage. The system seems to have aroused little resentment or worry, and indeed village life was so mechanical that there was little possibility of anyone becoming sensitive enough to think about incompatibility. True,

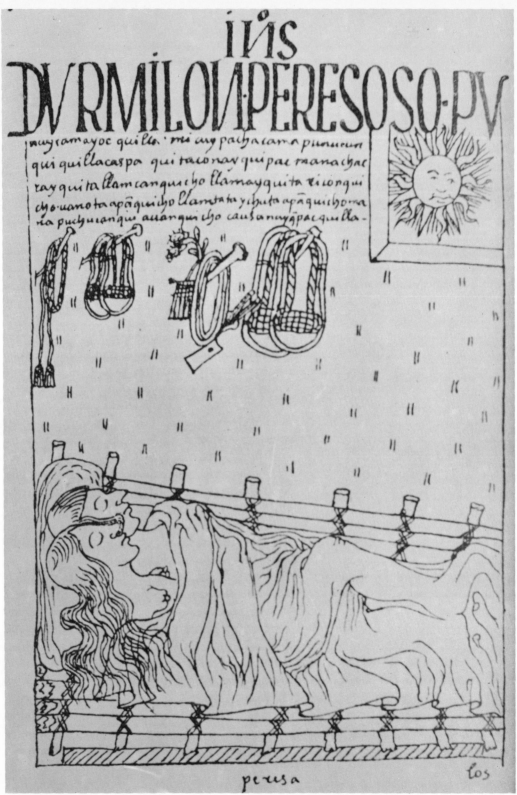

IVIS
DVRMILONPERESOSO·PV

muysamayoc quilla mi cuypachacama punucun
quiquillacaspa quitaconanquipac manachac
rayquita llamcanquiocho llamayquita ticonqui
chouanotaapāquiocho llamtatayhutaapāquichoma
ria puchucanqui auanquiocho causanuyñpacquilla·

perosa

los

A married couple

56

some of the surviving evidence tells of people falling in love, but that was a charming luxury for important people, as in the play of *Ollantay* where the course of true love even defied the Sapa Inca until the happy ending was reached.

All marriages were solemnized at one of the great seasonal festivals. When the reports of the village headmen were checked by the higher officials in the towns, all the young people of the right age were brought to the town for a communal ceremony. Their record strings were removed from their family *quipus* in the records of their villages. Then they were replaced by new strings which recorded the fact of the marriage and would later record the numbers of children and any alterations in the tributes and allowances appropriate for the newly formed family.

The village held a festal working party, and made a new house for the young couple, or, if there were more than one, a row of houses for all the pairs from the village. They also assigned old fields for them, or else everyone went to wall off a new section of land for their use.

The Inca *imperium* was a double structure, a series of family groups which were the basis from which upward selections were made by an oligarchy which radiated downwards from the focal point of a divine king. The mechanical basis of the whole structure was an excellent road system and an efficient organization of records. The intellectual side of it all was adaptation of an inheritance from the past made into the efficient instrument of a vast unifying force which was the concept of Tahuantinsuyu, the Four Quarters. This was conceived as something growing outwards from Cuzco to bring the benefit of good government to all of humanity who would accept the benevolence of the Sapa Inca, the earthly representative of the Sun.

Chapter Three

THE DIVINE SANCTIONS

The Sapa Inca was the closest living person in descent from his undying ancestor, the Sun God, Inti. Quilla, the Moon, was sister to the Sun. Therein lay the heavenly sanction for the Inca family. Yet the sun and moon and the stars, their children, were subject to immutable laws. They moved in their daily and seasonal rhythms, never failing and changing their relative positions with absolute regularity. There was a force which controlled them, and this was a personalized being, Actici Viracocha, the Holy and Religious Maker of the Universe. He was described by the wise men, the Amautas, as the breath which blew over the waters and brought life into being. His great temple was seventeen leagues outside Cuzco. It was unique in the highlands. So great a deity was in no need of any house on earth; the whole of the earth and the sky was the house of the Creator. There was an obligation for the Inca and all who were close to him to reverence Viracocha beyond all the other gods.

In the days of which we write the Incas had met the great gods of the coastal tribes, in particular a form of Viracocha as lord of the sea. He was Pachacamac, who constantly created the tremendous upsurge of life which everlastingly swept past the desert coasts. Everything that lived there was born of the breath of the wind and the foam of the sea. Long before Inca times the temple of Pachacamac (plate 18) was famous, for within the little house on top of its enormous mud brick pyramid was a figure of the god which gave oracular messages. In those days the little wooden figure with its seashell inlays was housed in a room filled with gold and silver vessels and hung with fantastic tapestries. Here the Creator spoke to his worshippers in the times of their distress. It seems that the oracle was singularly truthful and was so popular that when the Incas conquered the land they simply gave the god a name in their own Quechua language, and installed a Sun shrine in the courtyard to symbolize the Inca presence in the holy place.

There seems to have been little attempt by the Inca ruling class to impose any deep changes in local religions, so long as the captured peoples erected shrines to Inti and Quilla in a place a little higher than their old gods. It was different with Viracocha-Pachacamac. He was the Supreme One, respected equally by all civilized peoples. Nothing was ever done to reduce Viracocha to the level of the other gods, not even to the exalted position of Inti, the Sun.

There was a certain amount of difficulty with the coastal Chimu people about the position of the Sun God, but it was solved by giving the Sun a building beside the Moon temple. The principle of Sun worship was acceded to, but practice brought the Chimu people to sing hymns to the Moon. To them the Moon was a god of most wonderful power. He was named Sí (plate 3), and was symbolized by a silver figure of an animal wearing a moon-shaped silver helmet. It was of course the analogue of the almost universal idea of the "Rabbit in the Moon". Sí represented the cool of the night as opposed to the cruel heat of the sun on the burning desert coast. The Sun was a cruel deity to the Chimu, but Sí brought peace, and at regular intervals he shone over the dark ocean dispersing the daytime fogs and encouraging fishermen to reap rich harvests from the life of the sea. This seems to have been an ancient belief of the coastal Indians, probably based on their long habitation of the desert with the fruitful sea coast.

Among the Inca it was different. Their solar myths were part of the ancient inheritance of America which were shared with other peoples in many stages of civilization all the way from the primitive Eskimo upwards to the Inca.

The great temple of the Sun was in the heart of Cuzco. Here was the golden wall, which pictured the legend of the Sun. Here was the sacred emptiness in which the Inca was left alone at the winter solstice to welcome the return of his great ancestor to the rising path in the sky. Here also were the niches in the wall where the dead ancestors of the Inca were placed as beautifully preserved squatting mummies to partake of the glory of the great festivals. It was in the charge of the greatest official of the state, the Villac Umu, the High Priest. By virtue of his office the Villac Umu must be a relative of the Inca, usually a brother. The Sapa Inca exercized a careful choice from members of his family, because the office called for considerable intellectual ability and a knowledge of astronomy. The High Priest of the Sun was the keeper of the calendar and the ultimate

Chimu textile showing Viracocha-Pachacamac creating marine life

authority for adjustments between solar and lunar calendars in order to regulate the sequence of popular festivals. He also knew a good deal about popular religion throughout Tahuantinsuyu.

Around the courtyard of his simple and massive temple were shrines to the deities of all the peoples of the Four Quarters. They were attended by their own servants, but all were subservient to the Villac Umu. At festivals the deities were all brought out on litters and were carried by their priests as if they were the attendants to the golden image of the Sun.

Alas, the images of the gods are nearly all destroyed, but their nature can be deduced from smaller reliefs on pottery, and a few stone carvings. The image of Inti must have been very like the figure on the gate at Tiahuanaco, where he is shown dressed in a ceremonial tunic and crowned with a head-dress of lightning serpents which have alternate heads of pumas and condors. In his hand he holds great lightning serpents. There are tears on his cheeks; their meaning is no longer clear, but the Inca had a tradition that the tears of the Sun were the precious gold which they alone might wear. Around the Sun on this gateway are a number of winged figures which may well be the stars, flying like condors in a great flock every night across the sky, and there are other symbols on the borders which may refer to the wandering planets. There must have been something like this design in Ccoricancha. All we have is a drawing made by Don Juan de Santa Cruz Pachacuti-Yamqui Salcamayhua five generations after the Spanish conquest. This shows that the main figures on the wall were Sun, Moon, Rainbow and Thunder, while an empty space represented the ineffable quality of Viracocha. There were several star symbols which represented fairly accurately on the wall the groups of stars visible in the night sky on the day of the great Situa Festival in August.

Very little has been preserved which really explains Inca theology. It is obvious that the phenomena of the sky were very important, with Rainbow and Thunder associated with Sun, Moon, and Morning and Evening Star (the planet Venus) taking an important part. One can deduce a type of mythology not dissimilar from that of some of the North American tribes of the Great Plains. But how it was developed into ritual observance in so highly organized a country as Inca Peru is no longer clear. Two *quipus,* preserved in Göteborg, have been shown by Baron Erland Nördenskiold to contain astronomical calculations, but they are simply mute evidence that the necessary scientific knowledge existed, without any means of telling the legends which were associated with them.

From the Chimu area comes a legend which makes the Evening Star a kind of trickster-figure. There was a chief who had two very beautiful wives. The Evening Star came up, and managed to charm them so much that they both enjoyed intercourse with him while the chief was away. The chief returned and found his wives had been adulterous. He lay in wait and caught the Morning Star with them again. Then in accordance with ancient Peruvian custom he tied them all together and threw them over a cliff into the sea. Thus the great chief lost his wives and the Evening Star sank into the sea after the Sun, as he does every 520 days in the Venus cycle. The story is a fragment, but it is enough to let us understand that a great astronomical folklore once existed. Probably remnants exist to this day which might be recovered if anyone bothered to go to the remote villages with the humility to sit down to listen to the old people telling stories.

Side by side with the complex religion there were a thousand cults, of local deities,

60

Plate 6. Silver dish and gold beaker from coastal graves. They are standing on a appliqué cloth of Inca design. *British Museum. Photo: Derrick E. Wit*

Overleaf. Plate 7. Two views of a late Inca wooden *kero* inlaid with coloured masti *British Museum. Photo: Derrick E. Wit*

rocks and fountains, strange pinnacles on the mountains, the Kenko Stone (plate 16) and the rock of Hanacauri (who had been a brother of the first Inca). Even rivers and trees which had been linked in people's minds with stories of gods and spirits were revered. One can find many parallels to this in the stories of classical antiquity in Europe. The mass of the Peruvian people added to their religious beliefs the comfort which comes from lucky charms. Every unusual object was called *huaca,* which implied a mysterious spiritual quality attached to it. It might be something truly sacred like the mummy of a previous Sapa Inca, or just a lucky pebble, but whatever happened it was felt to be mysteriously effective. Like most of us, they never realized that the impulse to respect these things came from an unconscious desire to be in touch with a wider world of experience. People needed something more than a satisfactory material life. The *huacas* were expected to make their crops better, or make husbands or wives more charming. But they were accepted whether they proved effective or not because people had to find some way towards self-realization, even if it meant using such simple magic as collecting *huacas.* From the same impulse came the good living earned by soothsayers, necromancers, fortune-tellers and magicians of many kinds. These were not usually officials, but conducted their practice as a spare-time prestige activity.

Little is known about the magical practices of ancient Peru, except that in general outline they were startlingly like the magic practised in Europe of the same period. The planting of charmed objects in the path of an enemy, and the use of wood or wax figures, which were mutilated for destructive sympathetic magic, were prominent activities. There were people who forecast the future by the flight of birds, and who could hear the conversations of animals. Many divinatory methods were used such as burning strips of llama skin and watching how they moved, or dropping lucky pebbles and estimating the meaning of the patterns they made. Divination was much resorted to because people wanted to foretell their future. They were so secure that they became anxious.

The magicians were not greatly respected. They mostly dealt with minor events and filled a popular demand in much the same way as their fellows have done at all times and in all civilizations. What we should understand as the higher forms of magic were in the hands of the priesthood. The priests of the Sun not only arranged the calendar, but also conducted ceremonies at appropriate times to release the rains, or to dismiss the sins of individuals and communities. Their curse could kill, their blessing bring health. There is no evidence for abnormal suggestibility occurring among Peruvians; the power of magic was a matter of belief, and probability was rarely, if ever, put to the test.

A form of ceremonial magic existed in which symbols and numbers were used, but it was not recorded in sufficient detail for us to recreate any ceremony. In all probability it resembled many other systems in which the symbols are used to direct and canalize the will. It was probably almost a mechanism to aid thought projection.

Beyond the field of the magicians, and yet closely connected, came the medical profession. The doctors were men and women who had studied in the towns and particularly in the temples to gain proficiency. The healing art was recognized as a gift of the gods just as in the ancient world the spiritual gifts of Imhotep or Aesculapius were regarded as a necessary part of the soul of the medical man. Healing came from the powers of Earth and Sky, and so was ultimately derived from the boundless creator force, Viracocha. Earth supplied her herbs, and the Sun gave light and learning.

Plate 8. Silver gorget of pierced metal, in the form of a moon ship. 65
Private collection, Lima. Photo: George Holton

Plate 9. Stone bowl ground into shape and rubbed over with red pigment.
Photo: Derrick E. Witty

Demons and magician

66

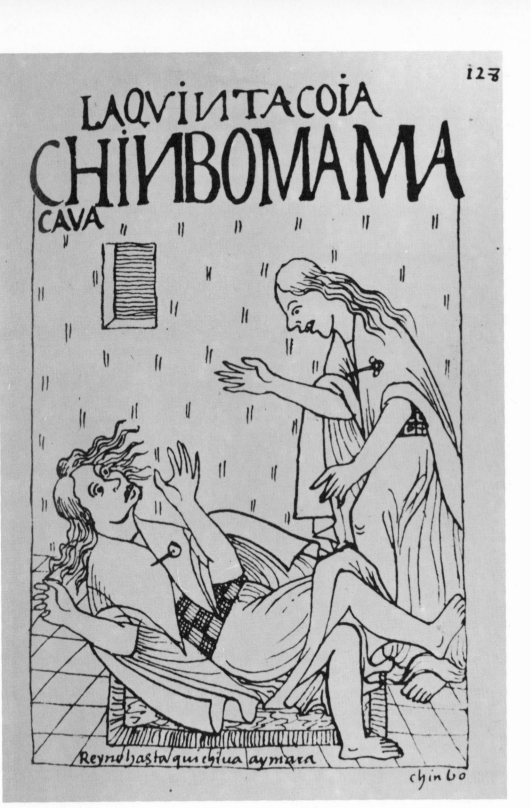

An epileptic seizure

Local spirit powers might be called upon by a healer. It was a good thing if he saw them as visions and received the assurance that they would guide him. These ecstatic experiences were projections from the unconscious mind and they usually found a form of manifestation which could be accepted by the consciousness. The normal human being does not easily accept the idea of inspiration from within. The ineffable words must be pronounced by an externally visualized divine being before they are accepted. That this attitude towards enlightenment was of great value in ancient Peru cannot be doubted. The healers were convinced that they would be helped and their own confidence must have greatly aided the patient. Their stock-in-trade was by no means primitive. They had a wide knowledge of herbal medicine, using herbs in a strictly scientific way. Details of cases were recorded, and the treatment and results discussed by the healers, who were loosely organized into local confraternities. A village might have but a single woman to heal all manner of sickness, but help was always available from any of her colleagues. It was not difficult to send messengers over the road system to the nearest temples where medical specialists could be found. Accounts of their work show that they were probably ahead of European medicine of the same period and that they were very highly trained within their own kind of collegiate discipline. The healers were part of the state organization and were supported with food and clothing from the official storehouses. A village medicine woman might only practise on rare occasions; but the community was responsible for assuring that her land was cultivated and her share of clothing was woven while she was occupied in her healing duties.

In some regions there were concentrations of specialists who were called upon for advice and treatment by many people. In the coastal mountains above the town of the oracle Rimac (now Lima) there was a tribal group known as the Yauyos who specialized in the treatment of injuries to the skull. Considering that slings and clubs were the favourite weapons of the Peruvians, there was obviously room for an endless succession of trained skull-menders to serve the state. Their training was extremely practical, and included methods of drugging the patients into insensibility and control of sensation by various nerve pressures. Their most famous activity concerned trepanning, by which portions of smashed or diseased bone were cut away from the skull. This was obviously a last resort, and was not by any means always successful. Nevertheless a number of skulls have been found in which the edges of the cut bone have grown successfully, and so provided evidence for years of life after the operation. Other surgery included removal of a torn spleen, cleaning out of ulcers, and the cleaning and after-care of wounds. Antiseptic treatment was not consciously employed, but the application of herbal washes and poultices might well have served this purpose.

Very sensibly, religion was involved in medical treatment. The healer knew the appropriate chants to call in spiritual powers to help the patient and was able to administer charms to be worn or displayed beside the patient. Many a sick Indian must have returned from the edge of death because of the acceptance of help which was symbolized by the charm and sung about in the chant. There was in this way a system of direct psychological aid to the sick as well as the occasional use of hypnosis.

Justice itself was a divine matter. The Sapa Inca was the representative of the Sun, he could do no wrong. Insofar as other members of the Inca extended family approached the holiness of the Sapa Inca, the possibilities of wrongdoing on their part were limited.

It was fully realized that apparent wrong might lead to right. They recognized that there was also a mischievous Spirit of Uncertainty which could reverse the nature of events. Yet on the whole the Inca family tried to live up to its position. If justice had to be invoked against a noble, it was secret and savage. For the non-Inca, tribal custom was the basic law and it was modified to fit the Inca system where necessary.

Basic codes were simple. Death was decreed for insulting the Sapa Inca, for adultery, theft, and murder. Extenuating circumstances were allowed to be brought in evidence, and this was particularly important in murder cases. The case was heard by a judge who was one of the higher civil servants. All the details were recorded on string *quipus* and kept for future reference. Within five days of the hearing the verdict was given. Sentence was executed immediately afterwards. If a later investigation showed that a judge had acted unfairly or had been bribed he would be killed and his family disgraced.

There was practically no civil litigation, since the social system did not presuppose individual rights to property, and so all torts against the person were regarded as offences against the state. A drunken fight was not uncommon, and was usually passed over unless the physical damage to one of the contestants incapacitated him from his share in the village work.

The reasoning behind the simple death sentences was that opposition to the Sapa Inca was denial of the organization given by the Sun himself; adultery was simply confusing the physical composition of the population and thus breaking Inca regulations; theft was taking from the Sun, the Inca, or the state-regulated individual, the goods which were decreed to them by the law; murder simply removed a work unit from the village records without the proper sanctions.

The laws about adultery were complicated by the allocation of the right to count one's quota of wives according to rank in the Inca aristocracy. The Sapa Inca had practically unlimited choice apart from his Ccoya. The other Inca nobles were allowed wives in proportion to their status, and this number was limited. In practice, the vast majority of the Inca family were as monogamous as the rest of the population.

The strictness of the marriage tie was a matter of civil order. The numbers of men and women were roughly equal. Specially attractive or skilled surplus members in a community could be diverted to the special services. No domestic quarrels were allowed to go far without the neighbours coming in to bring peace. In any case the normal routines of life kept women and men each in their own spheres of work for most of the day, and that made their personal contacts more pleasurable. The importance of marriage was that children were produced for the community, and the preservation of local tradition in an ordered form was assured.

In the towns there were young women who existed as a kind of guild for bringing peace to men. There is no parallel to them in modern civilization, but like the old-time Geishas they were regarded as respectable members of the community. Intercourse with them was not regarded as adultery. There was no chance that their children when brought into the lineage system of a village or town would confuse the recording system or provoke jealousies.

The highland tribes were of the opinion that the coast people were wildly immoral, and they were shocked by the occasional nakedness of the hot-land tribes.

On the whole, the attitudes to marriage and sex were simple and direct, and one gains the impression that most people accepted the national *mores* and found a properly balanced happiness without much complication of romance or sentiment.

Children were a delight. People were naturally kind to them. They were led gently through family tasks into the community. When a baby arrived the young parents earned tax exemption for a year. The birth was usually an affair for the women only, and the village medicine woman was aided by neighbours if necessary. The child was expelled from a squatting position, and sometimes the mother used a wooden bar to pull on. There were charms and herbs to help, and if there were special difficulties a runner could be sent for more skilled help from the specialists. The father had a magical part to play by keeping up a kind of respectable seclusion at the critical period. If a baby lost its mother while it was still tiny, a wet nurse could usually be found in the community. Sometimes a pap of flour was fed to the baby, but it was not a good substitute, and breast-feeding was practically universal. Naturally the mothers were very proud of their full breasts and not at all shy of suckling the child whenever it cried.

The most important social function of a child was to be recorded on the village *quipu*. From that moment it was entitled to its share of food, clothing, and land. Later on it would be given a very rudimentary grounding in necessary knowledge by the elders. If it was clever or beautiful there was the chance of selection for special service.

During the years of maturity, the person and the state were in full correspondence. The surplus of production was being delivered to the storehouses of the Sun and the Inca. Everything was recorded; the payments of the village or town quarter and the amounts of contributions as well as of allowances.

When old age came, the individual was still expected to produce food and clothing as part of a family unit within the community, but now the quotas expected were lower because it took more effort for the weakening organism to feed itself. Later on the flow was reversed and the state organization supplied extra food and clothing from the storehouses.

During the whole of life the individual had been involved in the greater life of the whole of Tahuantinsuyu, which was nourished by the divine powers and celebrated at the festivals of the moon and the four great solar festivals. Each year sins were driven away, the life of the nation was renewed, and the path of the Sun rose in the sky only to go down again as the year's end was attained. At last the cycle of individual life came to its end. The magicians and healers had no more power to avert the wonderful change. From Sapa Inca to captive servant, all must go.

It was not considered right to allow the body to be destroyed by the forces of decomposition. It must be at least partly preserved for the time when the personality revisited the earth. In the highland country, the viscera were removed and the body was taken to a mountain site where it could be put in a niche in the rocks to dry out in the antiseptic conditions of the extremely cold dry air. When it was properly dried it was bundled up in daily clothing and put away with the similarly dried bodies of the ancestors, either in a nearby cave or in a stone built tower, a *chullpa*, where the dried bodies were kept like cinerary urns in a Roman columbarium. In the hot coastlands the process was different. As before, the viscera were removed. But the body was dried on the hot sandy wastes, and washed over with a preservative lotion. It was then wrapped with many shirts and cloths and made into a bundle which was suitably interred in the desert sands.

70

Chimu child's shirt with shells representing red
and white fish

In the mountains most of the ancient bodies have disappeared. But from the coast the bodies hidden in the dry sand have been dug up, and now give us wonderful information about ancient times through their clothing, and through the pots and vessels which have been buried with them. They alone give us a real understanding of the tremendous living activity which was going on in ancient Peru. They turn the dry narratives, and even the occasional drawings, of the Spanish conquerors into something real. These graves have yielded up many secrets, but, alas, man has not respected the bodies of the dead except when they have been preserved in museums. The care of the Incas for the dead has not been echoed by materially-minded modern man.

The Sapa Incas and their Ccoyas were also dried and treated with special preservatives. They were very perfectly preserved, brown and dry, with every hair in place. Each Sapa Inca was kept in a special room in the palace which he had built for his lifetime. One never knew when Father Sun would send back the soul of one of his children, so the palace of a past Sapa Inca was kept in running order with its complement of servants and workers, its share of the royal income and constant supplies of fresh food and clothing. On the throne the bodies of the Sapa Inca and Ccoya sat squatting peacefully with bowed heads as if in meditation. On the great festivals of the Sun the ancient Sapa Incas were carried in procession. People adored them as they would the living Sapa Inca, and many openly wept to see the painted boards which depicted the great events of their glorious past. There was nothing gruesome about this cult, it was a logical part of the

71

belief in the sun kings, and everything connected with it was made as reverent and beautiful as possible. Death was not hidden; it was part of human experience, and even the holy Sapa Incas took part in it.

After death the Incas were present in a special way in the heaven of the Sun, and the spirits of their family had some kind of share in it. There was a rather vague underworld for the souls of the majority of people. Some of the vases of the coastal peoples show the dead as skeletons dancing and apparently enjoying a very happy life. There are few legends preserved for us to explain all this. There seems to have been little sense that earthly behaviour might condition the nature of the future existence.

We have no reason for thinking that the hopes of a future existence among the Peruvian Indians of Inca times were any greater than those experienced by the Babylonians or the Greeks. There was the same spirit of stoicism in the face of life and acceptance of death. All these cultures attained to glorious achievement in practical affairs. The Peruvians achieved a certain splendour of thought in the concept of Viracocha, which amounted to a kind of monotheism in that he was the power behind the gods, and was conceived as a sentient being.

Perhaps more than most peoples the Peruvians under Inca rule lived a life fully integrated between material affairs and religious sanctions. In that we may find a reasonable explanation of the success of the civilization. It was a complete entity, almost as if Tahuantinsuyu were a supra-personality. The end came when the true Inca, Huascar, was no longer able to control the organic whole. The treachery of Atahuallpa was almost as if a schizophrenic attack had caused paralysis. But, in the earlier time of which we are writing, the lands of the Sapa Inca were at their most vigorous growth and the social structure was well organized and running efficiently.

Plate 10. Part of a wooden *paccha* inlaid with patterns in mastic. *Chicha* was poured into the bowl, and trickled out of the mouth of the man being attacked by a giant puma. It then ran down grooves in the *paccha* into the mouth of the drinker. Mounted on Chimu tapestry. *British Museum. Photo: Derrick E. Witty*

Chapter Four

SOCIAL LIFE

In the time of Topa Inca Yupanqui the country had reached its utmost brilliance. The Sapa Inca himself made many journeys to inspect his provinces. He visited every town, and stayed in the palaces which were kept ready for such ceremonial visits. Sometimes he sought relaxation in such places as the beautiful valley of Yucay where warm country plants grew in the setting of the mountains. Here was a cold spring which was channelled through golden spouts into a silver bath for the Sapa Inca. This was a place for the pleasant things of life; the fruits and drink made from maize chewed by the perfumed mouths of favourite wives; the lovely delicacy of the Chumpi cloth woven for the royal family; and of course the women of the court who were ruled over by the Ccoya herself. Yet even here there was no relaxation of law and routine. The Inca was never free. Even in moments of the most intense enjoyment he was a sacred being guarded by his palace servants. When the great nobles came to visit him they came wearing deliberately simple clothes, and each bore a little package on his back to show that he was but a slave of the Sapa Inca.

Life was similar for the Ccoya, who had her separate suite of rooms and her team of beautiful maids. She also was a holy being, and was associated with silver in the life of the nation. She exercised a great deal of personal power. Although the chronicles tell us of the quality of the Ccoya as a person, we know little of her life as the queen bee of this extraordinary hive.

However, it was Topa Inca Yupanqui who led his armies as far as the river Maule in Chile, and who went by balsa into the wide Pacific Ocean on a journey which lasted for some months. It is thought that he may have visited the Paumotu Islands or some neighbouring Polynesian group, since the oral tradition described a crowded land populated by dark skinned people who had wavy hair.

While the Sapa Inca was away on such journeys it was not the Ccoya who was the chief representative of state, but her son, and a council of the leading nobles. Her position was very similar to that in the old Ashanti kingdom where the queen mother held a spiritual leadership which did not outwardly interfere with the secular power wielded by her son.

The great sea adventure had no consequences for Peruvian history, though it must have brought a new understanding of legends about previous visitors from the west. The regular trade up and down the coast was conducted by balsas travelling one way with the winds, and then furling sails and dropping the centre boards to drift back northwards with the Humboldt Current. On these rafts heavy cargoes were carried, and passengers also travelled on them between coastal towns. It was a slower but more pleasant route than the great road across the wastelands.

Plate 11. Group of small hard-stone vessels in characteristic Inca forms.
British Museum. Photo: Derrick E. Witty

75

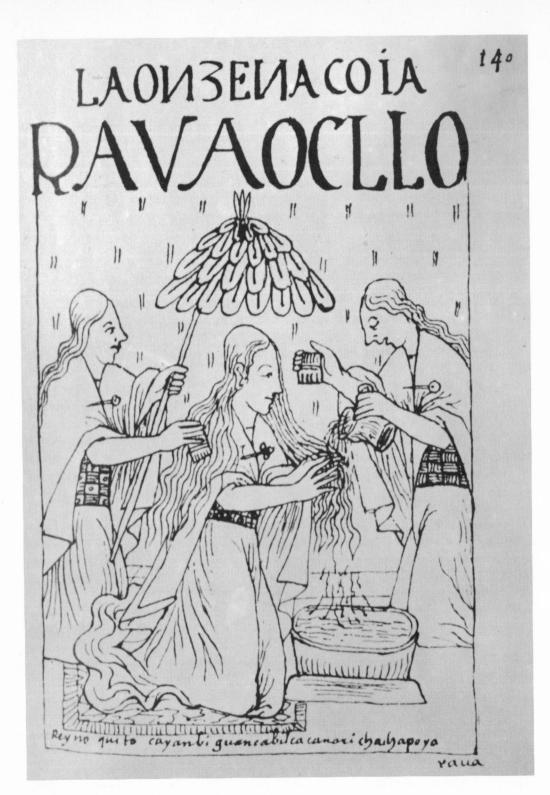

LAONZENACOIA
RAVAOCLLO

Reyno quito cayanbi guancabilca canori chachapoyo

yana

The Ccoya at her toilet

76

Model of a balsa raft

An advance of the army to the south was the cause of an enormous extension of the roads of Peru. Topa Inca Yupanqui needed a safe path for the troops to pass and for llama caravans to carry goods to the newly assimilated territories, so levies of workmen were called up to form another army of construction workers. The work was efficiently done, but for some time the towns of Peru seemed even quieter than usual.

Towns had originated in Peru long before Inca times. They were situated in areas which were not cultivable but where there was easy access to fertile land and to communication routes. It was natural that when the Inca government perfected the road system the towns should remain at nodes in the network. They were also made into administrative centres, so new buildings were often added, including a palace for the Sapa Inca to visit on the occasions of his royal progress. The towns were usually the repositories of the state storehouses, and every town included a temple to Inti, the Sun God. This was a centre of learning and teaching.

Most accounts describe the towns as strangely silent. People gathered together but the soft tread of their sandalled feet, and the complete absence of any wheeled vehicle, gave new value to the softer sounds of human speech and song. There was an immense difference between highland and coastal towns, but the quietness was universal. It was broken at festival times by music and song and much shouting. The people had a

Harvest festival

gift for their own gentle music played by panpipes of many different sizes, whistles, and wooden trumpets. There were wooden gongs, and hundreds of little tambours tapped in rhythm by the women. One cannot describe this music well. Much of it has survived among the Indian villages in the mountains, but the only way to understand it is through recordings of the strange sad sweetness of sound and the gentle visceral rhythms.

The lunar farming festivals were gay affairs in which everyone from town or village who could help in digging the ground or reaping the crops performed his part. Agriculture was a matter between humanity and the gods, and was therefore joyful. The rituals called for help or gave thanks for help received. All the people of a village were praying together on these occasions, and most people in the towns were similarly concerned with the ceremonies for the very good reason that they too had to grow the food they consumed and produce a proper surplus for the Sun and the state.

Everyone was present at the Sun temple for these occasions. The buildings were often quite small, a rectangular hall with an apsidal end, and in the courtyard was a stepped stone rather like a throne which acted as a gnomon for recording the length of the shadow cast by the sun from day to day at noon. This stone was indeed a throne, an *Intihuatana*, Seat for Inti the Sun Lord (plate 15). The festivals always lasted for at least two days so that the ceremonial observances could be followed by a celebration of the whole populace who danced and sang, and drank their fresh brewed *chicha*, until exhaustion joined with intoxication laid them to rest wherever they happened to fall.

The great Sun festivals were at once more festive and more solemn. The very important ones were held in November when the sun passed nearly overhead at Tiahuanaco (surprisingly not at Cuzco) and when it was on its way north over the equator, at the equinox. But the greatest of all festivals was in late June. Then the divine Sun was lowest in the northern sky, and it was time that his children must purify themselves in readiness for him to make his accustomed return.

The June solstice festival was called *Intip Raymi*. It was preceded by the Situa, or cleansing feast. For three days before the feast the nation was in mourning. All fires were put out and only a fasting diet was permitted. The sins of the nation were solemnly brought by magic to Cuzco and were implanted in a scapegoat, a black llama. The leading younger Inca men drove the beast out of the city and across the river in the valley. As it raced away into the mountains to await its fate people recited their sins and bundled them up into parcels of wood and straw which were sent floating down the river. So the world of mankind was purified and bad luck and sickness driven away from Tahuantinsuyu for the coming year. A similar ceremony was carried out in every town of the country, but in Cuzco the really great magical power was wielded, because it was the navel of the earth, the centre beloved of the Sun.

After the Situa there were great processions, and in Cuzco the Sapa Inca, the Ccoya and the Villac Umu led the nobles in a dawn procession. This wonderful ceremony started on 21 June when the first rays of the sunrise shone on to the golden wall inside Ccoricancha and found the Sapa Inca alone in the great stone hall lined for the occasion with the seated mummies of his ancestors. That morning once in the year was the only time when the Sapa Inca could be alone with his god. As the Sun burst in, the Sapa Inca put on his head-dress and sandals and was joined by the power of the nation expressed

EL PRIMERO MES DE ENERO.
CAPACRAIMICAMAI
quilla

penetencia y ayunos del ynga

papaq

The Situa, or cleansing festival

80

The festival of *Intip Raymi*

in the persons of the great nobles and the élite of the army. The citizens of Cuzco joined in the procession dressed in tunics of different colours which divided those of Upper and Lower Cuzco from each other. The holy mummies of the dead Sapa Incas were carried in the procession, and following them the gods of the subject tribes were borne on litters by their local chiefs. The procession finally returned to the great square in front of Ccoricancha. There the parties were formed into groups. A pure white llama clad in red and gold harness was sacrificed for the Sun. Then others were killed to make a feast for the people. The Sapa Inca provided thousands of vases of fresh-brewed *chicha* as a symbol of fruitfulness in the crops and peace among the people. On one occasion it is said that Topa Inca Yupanqui, in a fit of care for his people, reduced the size of the vessels in which the *chicha* was distributed. The result was public dissent which nearly amounted to a strike. Never before had a Sapa Inca been so nearly faced with a popular uprising. So the next year he returned the permitted quantity of *chicha* to the old measures and allowed the people to get as stupidly drunk as they liked.

After a week of festivities and processions the town was cleaned, and all the strangers, who had been sent to camps outside Cuzco during the festival, were allowed to return to the great sacred city of the Sun once more.

In the great festivals like the Situa the Sapa Inca really came into contact with his people. He presided at the ceremonies, and while the greatest respect was shown it was not compulsory for everyone to throw themselves face downwards on the ground when he passed by. The Sapa Inca was the earthly representative of the Sun passing among the stars.

There was no middle class in Peru, unless one counts the officials as such. They worked normally in the provincial capitals, keeping records and administering services. Their allowances of food and clothing were good and they held a position of dignity recognized by the people. That was the real nature of social reward in Peru. No one held private property, and no community within Tahuantinsuyu worked except for the benefit of the whole organism. The Inca system of keeping the communities distinct from one another was for ease of organization, but it also made quite sure that there was no chance of a large section of the population seceding and so destroying the work of the Sapa Inca and his divine ancestors.

Manufactures were planned on a locality basis, but true factory workshops were attached to all the cities. Into these were sent drafts of women to work preparing thread and weaving cloth to established patterns. They used only the normal primitive back-strap loom with no kind of mechanization. Working to a regular rhythm under the direction of overseers, they produced the great quantities of cloth needed for the storehouses of the Inca. The Inca organizers, working to their usual plan, simplified the number of patterns woven, and for most purposes demanded a plain chequer pattern. This simplification of design made production easier. There was no urge to increase the amount of production, for that was all planned in advance, but simplification meant that work took less energy and the production was easier and happier.

One suspects that pottery was also the product of organized workshops, for in the highlands the Inca-period ceramics bear a very limited series of decorations, and all are comprised within six types of form.

The workshops were local institutions. There is evidence that, long before the time

Country people spinning thread

Woman weaving

84

of the Incas, weavers were spending the time when they were not working in the farms, in the manufacture of textiles to prescribed patterns.

However, there were specialized crafts which demanded more than usual knowledge and ability. In particular, the metalworkers were specialists of standing. Presumably they were fully employed in their work for most of the year, and were supported by food and clothing from the storehouses of the Inca. There must have been a corporate attitude and even craft guilds among fellow craft workers, but in normal life they lived in the local villages and towns and took part in the festivals with their neighbours.

The daily routine of life was quite simple among all groups of people. The morning meal was light, and during the day little was eaten. The evening meal was the main one of the day. Food was reasonably mixed. Llama meat was fairly easy to come by, and at festival times selected male beasts were slaughtered for food. The staple food was, however, starch obtained from maize, quinoa, or potatoes, according to the district. Everywhere there were varieties of beans which were much prized as seasonal foods. Fruits grew in the highlands, but the cultivated tropical fruits were naturally more important on the coast. The highlanders obtained some of this type of food by exchange with the Indians of the great Amazon forests. Groundnuts were a coastal product. Tropical spices were an article of trade. The normal diet of the people was palatable and nourishing, though interchange between regions was slight. Many women must have known how to vary the mixture to keep their families interested. The basic dishes were flat griddle cakes of grain, and thick stews of beans. Meat or fish added variety.

The house of the common people on the highlands was a foursquare room with a thatched roof. On the coasts it was an adobe structure with a cotton awning. On the coast, fires were lit only in the courtyard outside the house. In the highlands, fires were often kept indoors to warm the room, but great care was taken because of the dry and very thick thatch on the roofs. The family slept on mats in their appropriate corners. There was no attempt at privacy; because all activities were natural, they felt that there was little need for modesty.

Women usually went to live in little huts during their menstrual periods away from the home, but this was really a magical protection. It may well have arisen from the natural emotional situations of the period, and was therefore wise and helpful to life in the family. Such regulations were not made by Inca law, but seem to have arisen here, as in many other parts of the world, from the natural good sense of savages who realized the essential needs of social life.

On the whole, the ancient Peruvian Indians were a cleanly people. It was important to them to have their homes well swept out and their clothes kept clean. They prided themselves on the beauty of their hair and the quality of their complexions. This was just as true of the men as the women. There was a general social pressure towards good order which made it difficult for the lazy and feckless to disgrace their neighbourhood, and in any case they were always in danger of being helped by their neighbours. This was not so kindly as it sounds, because there was often a bitter whip in the songs which accompanied the work. It was felt that a bad home reflected bad work in the fields and so meant that everybody in the community had to work a bit harder to make up the production quotas imposed on them.

When, however, there were cases of real inability to cope with life, they were seen as a visitation of the spirits because of some evil committed in the past, and the sufferers were cared for officially. Really crazed people were pitied and fed; while people hoped that some remark made by them would be of oracular significance, as it might well happen to be, because they lived only in their unconscious minds. A strange regulation condemned sub-normal youths to marry only sub-normal girls. The theory was that like must mate with like. It may have helped the unhappy traits to become stable within a narrow group. Of course the children born of sub-normal parents would be carefully watched and selected for separate service if they were normal in behaviour. With state selection in this way, the Mendelian elements in the situation would have been emphasized, and probably the deficiency was kept within limits. Certainly we hear little of any bad mental balance in the Indians at the time of the Spanish invasion. The people deteriorated later under the peonage system.

Slavery was not common in Peru. Certain captives might become forced labourers in army service, but this was a local and temporary servitude. There was a class of professional servants of low social status, who were fed and clothed by the nobles who used their services. They were said to have been descendants of rebellious tribes in the past, but these Yanaconas in the times of the greater Sapa Incas were more probably simply children whose circumstances separated them from normal family life and so became something like wards of state. They were by no means helpless or ill-treated. The Inca system never developed to the point where such retainers could become anything like a corps of Janissaries, or the personal retainers of a medieval European warrior chief. However, the seeds of such development were present.

Apart from the lonely shepherds who looked after the immense herds of llamas and alpacas on the high plateaus, there were few Peruvians who were not impressed for labour service on the road system. This was a communal responsibility, and each village or town was responsible for the upkeep of local roads. The universality of the road system has been well shown by the recent researches of Victor von Hagen, who has proved that the old accounts of a maze of cross-roads linking the main highways were the literal truth. Tahuantinsuyu probably possessed the best communications system of any nation in the days before mechanical transport was invented.

An element of local pride was involved in keeping the highways clear. The hardest work fell on the coastal peoples who had to contend with desert sand. The trail was marked by large wooden posts on either side of the roadway. Although a rough paving was achieved by the use of stones and pebbles, and even matting, the real problem was to keep the trail reasonably clear of soft, wind-blown sands. This meant the occasional turnout of large numbers of men for duties of digging out the trail and piling sand on either side, so as to leave the lines of posts quite clear and the basic surface hard enough to walk over successfully. They had performed this work for their own purposes long before the Inca conquest, but one can understand why they developed the sailing balsa as the means of transport preferred beyond all others.

In the grim conditions of the coast, all work was performed in the cool of the day, and when the middle week of each moon arrived a great deal could be done by moonlight. As was usual with all group activities the start and finish of a task was accompanied by a good deal of festivity. Dancing and drinking made a welcome change from the work songs which had to fill the intervening days of heavy labour.

GOVERNADOR DE LOS CAMINOS REALES
CAPAC ÑAN TOCRICOC ALITA
INGA

Planning the course of a road

Above. A section of Inca road in the coastal desert *(photo: Victor von Hagen)*

Below. A section of Inca road on the slopes of the Andes *(photo: Victor von Hagen)*

In the mountains the upkeep of the roads was less arduous. The traffic was not destructive to road surfaces. Llama caravans, and the passage of armies with sandalled feet, made little impression on the rocks, but there were occasional landslides, and every now and then widespread destruction from earthquakes which might even cause a section of the highway to need re-routing. In such abnormal conditions help would be forthcoming from the army.

It was a straightforward task to light a fire on a big rock and then douse the hot surface with water in order to start cracks. Then wooden wedges were inserted and soaked with water so that their expansion would rive the rock apart. When the process was simultaneously performed by hundreds of groups working on a stretch of road the speed of the clearance seemed quite incredible. The secret of road construction lay not so much in advanced technology as in superb organization.

There was good reason for celebrating such accomplishments by a festival. It was a real incentive to the local people to find that their spell of intense effort was accorded public recognition by a festival specially arranged from the storehouses of the Inca. In a world without personal power, and a singular lack of privilege, the group festivity was the highest of enjoyments, and the individual found that the possibility of displaying his personality among his fellows on equal terms of happiness was very agreeable.

The social aspect of state service was never lost sight of by the Inca administration. Community pride was used as a spur to excellence, through the competition to produce good quality work between adjacent communities. The isolation of groups was maintained, however, by the system of local responsibility. The only journeys made by most villagers were to the local town when they went to the markets and ceremonies. Wider travels occurred for men only through a small part of life during the period of military service. The system of local district apartness with equality was most efficient and seems to have satisfied most of the population. Young people with wanderlust might have a chance, apart from the army, by becoming selected for administrative service, which was fairly easy since the majority of any age group would be lacking in the initiative to advance.

Some of the young men graduated to the professions which we have already described, but some specialized as architects. They worked from scale models, making first a site model in clay, and then designing the single-storey courtyard buildings to fit into the site, with an eye to beauty as well as convenience. The simple and massive forms of Inca architecture were unrelieved by any ornament, except sometimes rows of niches with inward-sloping sides to carry out the pattern of doorways. Sometimes interior buildings, such as storehouses, were made circular. Every building in the highlands was covered by a thick roof of thatch.

The architect had to know where suitable stone could be quarried and decide on the method of construction, whether to adopt the military type of building with the largest possible stones, or the more elegant structures of small rectangular blocks laid in regular fitted courses. In general, the edges of blocks were slightly bevelled inwards so as to show the shape of the stones. But the joints were ground down to make fits of great accuracy so that the blocks were as secure as if cemented together. The earthquake shocks, which were frequent events, simply made the stones jump up a little and then fall back into place. The Inca system of building was as nearly earthquake-proof as anything invented

Festival dance

in modern times. The aesthetic of the architect was concerned with simple mass and surface quality. There was no desire to exhibit elegance or curious fantasy. The perfect fitness of absolute simplicity was the aim. It seems to have often produced works of great power and beauty, though altogether lacking in charm. Even the magnificent Ccoricancha, of which the lower walls and apse still survive, was quite without ornament. The power of this holy of holies depended simply on mass and proportion aided by the quality of the stone used and the perfection of the fitting which was not embellished in any way. This was craftsmanship in the service of an architecture determined by an exacting taste.

Since architecture was so specialized a profession, there was considerable mobility. A specially favoured master would be commanded to work in many cities of Tahuantinsuyu, not only within his own area. The real division was geographical. Good highland architecture was utterly unsuitable for coastal conditions, just as the adobe constructions of the coastlands would crumble into dust and mud in the mountains.

The coastal people liked more decoration and built their mud bricks into patterns which copy their textile design. It was easy to carve the adobe surfaces, and the designs in that almost rainless land remained sharp for centuries. There was a great deal of colour painted on over a white lime-wash undercoating. This art sometimes reached a level which can only be described as fresco painting, though the work consisted of flat

Plate 12. Machu Picchu, on a mountain surrounded by higher peaks flanking th
Urubamba valley. The *andenes* or cultivation terraces in the foregroun
are among the best-preserved of their kind. *Photo: Victor von Hag*

Inca trapezoidal niche *(photo: Victor von Hagen)*

monochrome geometrical forms. The coastal architects had these things to consider as well as simple form, but they never achieved the severe beauty of the highland works of architecture.

The basic house was a single room, and as the design advanced socially it multiplied itself. The organization of a palace was simply a series of courtyards surrounded by single-room apartments. Some of these were used as workshops, some as storehouses, others as living quarters for officials and servants. The quarters of the Sapa Inca and Ccoya were as simple as the other rooms, but large in size and decorated with a profusion of embroideries and gold and silver ornament. Such a palace structure reflected the simple divisions of social life. It was in effect a kind of positional social notation, not unlike the knots on a *quipu* which indicated values in a decimal notation by their position on the string.

The architect designed and watched over the great stone constructions for public service. The villagers put up their own simple structures of clay-mortared stones. In any region there was a place for people to live in, and that was a very simple rectangle of walls with a doorway and very rarely with any window. Above was the thatch, and there the smoke from wood fires hung in black wreaths which were cleared away when the thatch was renewed. No other type of house could evolve from this simple basic element

ate 13. The layout of part of the town of Machu Picchu. Note the steep angles the roofs once covered with heavy thatch, and the Sun temple crowning a nearly ramidal rock at the foot of the highest peak. *Photo: Stephen Harrison*

93

The ruins of Machu Picchu

in any part of Peru, because there was no demand for more complex structures or for the erection of great towers except in a few fortresses. Life was lived in one room or in the open air. Staircases were made for roads, not for interior access to layers of rooms. Perhaps that was wise in an earthquake-troubled country.

House furnishing was extremely simple. There were plenty of baskets for containing cloth and weaving materials. Boxes of various kinds stood around the walls. Often these were prettily carved, and were sometimes decorated with lacquer pictures. They were used for holding more precious personal things, necklaces, silver pins, and so on. The pottery stood on the floor, supported by coiled stands of grass or skin. Mats were sometimes used, but the hard beaten and polished earthen floors were usually very clean. People slept on mats with a simple coverlet. They did not feel any desire for much more comfort. There were occasional box beds with a stuffing of wool and straw for very old people, but the bed was not normal furniture, and neither was there any table or chair. Meals were eaten from platters on a mat, while the family squatted around on mats or low cushions. Father ate first, and the women and babies followed on. In the big houses there were low bench-like tables, and thicker cushions to squat on. Usually food was cut before cooking. The *tumu* knife was not very useful as a table implement. Spoons were used, but not forks. Fingers were washed in little bowls between courses.

The Sapa Inca never used a bowl twice, and fed from silver and gold. The peasant used a little pottery dish or a plaited mat, both made by his wife. Yet the routine of a meal was just the same, and in all families conversation was regarded as an agreeable accompaniment to the meal. In fact, at least among the Quechua-speaking highland peoples, there was pleasure in the elegant use of the language, and both poetry and jokes were considered worth while. A Peruvian evening at home was not a dull affair at all.

It is strange that we know so little of the ordinary life of the people in Inca times. The reason is mostly that the Inca people displayed a stern dislike of representational art. The few surviving legends and tales give a picture of a basically gay people who did not take life as seriously as their architecture would lead one to think. The excellence of home-made textiles and ceramics shows that there was a creative happiness available for most people.

Pictures drawn by Huaman Poma de Ayala, a generation after the conquest, show his childhood in a world which still clung to Inca family tradition. These indicate the care which was given to the education of children by their parents, and the interest in each other's welfare taken by relatives of at least three generations. There were frequent social calls and a lot of discussion was carried on about the events of everyday life. All visitors were treated with ceremonial politeness, as elaborate in its own way as the courtesy of the Spaniards. Children listened to all conversation and so learned of life, and thereby grew into the community. The poverty and gloom of life among the Indians of nineteenth and early twentieth century Peru did not exist under the Incas. The atmosphere was perhaps a little fatalistic, but gaiety was as much part of fate as suffering. When suffering came there was a social consciousness which brought aid from the neighbours. We should also remember that the same social consciousness forced the Sapa Inca to provide sufficient strong drink for the festal intoxication after the dancing and singing of the gay festival of the returning Sun.

Chapter Five

THE EXPANSION OF THE FOUR QUARTERS

Tahuantinsuyu was no vague dream concept. It had an exact geographical significance to the Incas. The reference was to the northern mountains, the eastern fringe of the great forest, the southern mountains and deserts towards Chile, and the western ocean coasts. In all these directions the Inca power had made contact with other peoples. In most cases it was clear that there would be great benefits to the strangers if they could be brought into contact and eventually absorbed within the unity of Tahuantinsuyu.

There was a certain amount of trade, but, as we have noticed already, Tahuantinsuyu was a very efficient self-supporting unit. There was little which needed to be imported, but it was naturally of interest. From the great ocean there were few contacts with new peoples, once the kingdom of the Chimu had been absorbed. Polynesian legends tell of a visit from the Marquesas Islands in the twelfth century which apparently reached the Chimu cities before the Inca conquest. Some of the voyagers returned home with a wonder story. Did such stray voyages bring the coconut or sweet potato to Peru? Then in the mid twentieth century the late Father Castellví reported a tribe with curly hair in the forests of Colombian Amazonia who spoke a dialect with a large proportion of Malayo-Polynesian words. One immediately thinks of them as descended from *mitimaes*, transported from the coastal lowlands, whose origin was probably from a canoe expedition. On the other hand the voyage of Topa Inca Yupanqui suggests that the Peruvians had a good idea of the possibility of reaching inhabited lands in the great ocean. But these contacts both ways were small in extent though it is certain that contacts were made and some slight cultural exchanges achieved. There is, however, no evidence of determined trading voyages or regular contacts between the two very dissimilar races. The wide ocean to the west was not an open pathway for the Inca power.

To the north there was a powerful kingdom controlled by the Cara people of Ecuador. There was reason for trade here, partly for the importation of emeralds from Colombia and partly for the use of the coastal forest lands which produced the balsa trees necessary for building the great rafts which were employed in coastwise transport in Tahuantinsuyu. At the time of Topa Inca Yupanqui there were occasional frontier skirmishes, but the real stride forward to capture the Cara kingdom was not undertaken until his son led the armies. No doubt the absorption was considered, but the superiority of the Inca power was not yet overwhelming.

The southern lands were of most interest to the Sapa Inca. It may be that his determination to take them over had some connection with an irruption of the Diaguita tribes who lived in the lands where the Andes bordered the Argentine pampas. Their armies had broken through to control the Chilean coast. In any case, the land was already in contact with Peru, which imported a pleasant semi-precious stone which was

Marquesan bamboo armlet with decoration that
seems to resemble Peruvian art

a blue variety of copper carbonate, not unlike turquoise in appearance. There were also plentiful supplies of copper and tin to be obtained from northern Chile as well as stones for jewellery. Trade could have continued by balsa raft quite easily, but when it was decided to acquire the territory for Tahuantinsuyu there was a need to extend the great highway systems to the south. This was done successfully, and the Inca borders reached the Atacama Desert and were fixed for the time being at the river Maule. There was never a permanent settlement of frontiers for Tahuantinsuyu; its mission was to spread outwards to bring all places eventually within the four quarters of the imperium of the Sun.

The forests of the east were a source of much trade with the comparatively small groups of Indians. Great quantities of feathers, bamboo, and tropical fruits were brought in. Occasionally the wild tribesmen made a foray into the highland country, but they were usually cut off by garrisons moving across their line of retreat in the foothills of the mountains. The Peruvian town garrisons would then drive them back into the trap. The climatic change in any case usually weakened the enthusiasm of the forest warriors, who were more interested in plunder than in actual conquest. It was not Inca policy to enter the forests to any great extent. Experience had taught them that their armies were not immune to the fevers of the hot lands, and their trading convoys had encountered no peoples which could constitute a threat to the stability of Tahuantinsuyu. There seems to have been a road along the Andean foothills with a regular chain of fortress villages, but even in Inca times this was becoming overgrown and losing importance. It was better for all concerned that the forests should remain deep jungle, and the tribes slowly acculturate until they could be accepted into Tahuantinsuyu. Meanwhile, their dances were admired and their feathers worn with much real pleasure. Even today some of the Jivaro and their neighbours can weave cloth which still echoes the ancient techniques of Inca times.

Trade was a state business, and the transport of goods into the towns was organized by the town commanders. The material was used for official purposes by the jewellers, feather-workers, boat builders and so on. These things were all pleasing additions to a self-sufficient economy and were given official encouragement. The Incas never had to fight a war for trade. Nowhere did they organize the phenomenon of the commercial mission which was an excuse for armed robbery. The desire for power was there, and it had the best of all excuses — the benefit of the conquered people.

The Inca were at an extraordinary stage of civilization. In the fifteenth century A.D. they had an advanced Bronze Age technology. In Europe the development of the Bronze Age meant the break-up of cultural groups into smaller, more active, states each with its chief of divine descent and each with a determination to plunder its neighbours. There was a fall of real culture with the arrival of new technologies. The same thing happened in most other parts of the world, though China seems to have advanced in culture and established larger units. But the Inca turned the technological advance to the development of unification rather than to the development of fierce struggles for independence.

Among more primitive types of human communities this point in technological development was probably the key point in the development of national consciousness. The Inca tried to create a supra-national state, Tahuantinsuyu, but their experiment

Indians of the Amazon forest

The capture of Sapa Inca Huascar

100

broke down just before the Spaniards arrived with their version of late Iron Age barbarism. The seizure of Huascar Inca marked the fall of unified Inca direction before individualist power-seekers. They had begun to tread the road followed by the rest of humanity, and, terrible as it was, the Spanish conquest may have saved them from centuries of painful and murderous dynastic confusions of the medieval European type. At least the Spaniards brought a better theoretical concept of the individual and a respect for Roman Law. If they had known the truth, they had a better religion, but like most people they shaped their religion to suit their greed, which was an unhappy thing for Peru.

The Inca policy was so bound up with the cultural state of their time that we can almost imagine that we are looking at a culture of some three thousand years earlier in the Middle East. Yet it displayed ideas about social organization which were of a type suited more to a great technocracy than to a primitive kingship of the pharaonic type.

The military force at the disposal of the Sapa Inca was conditioned by the technological state of the country. The sling was the most deadly projectile weapon. Spear, long-handled axe and bronze-headed mace were the effective weapons. Protection was afforded by a wooden helmet covered with bronze, long quilted tunic and flexible quilted shield. The speed of the army was the common jog-trot of the Peruvian mountaineer which enabled them to travel many hours at a time keeping a pace of about three miles an hour. The soldiers carried only their own accoutrements, and an army of porters carried the baggage slung on their backs by a tump line round their foreheads. Llama transport was neither fast enough nor strong enough for the army. All this simplicity was made into a power worthy of a great nation by the excellent system of storehouses along the roads and an efficient and strikingly modern commissariat. As usual, the efficiency of the supply organization depended on messengers who carried the necessary information and requests coded up on the knotted string *quipus*.

The high command was theoretically a preserve of the Inca family, but it was not necessarily so. The army commanders could be quite as easily selected from the ranks provided that they displayed unusual ability and determined devotion to the Sapa Inca. Such great persons were easily accepted into the Inca clan by marriage with some suitable junior princess selected from among the Sun Maidens. Only one ·fortress was garrisoned solely by the Inca family, and this was the key fortress overlooking Cuzco itself. It was called the Sacsahuaman (plate 2), the hawk's eyrie, and remains largely complete today with the exception of the interior buildings and the famous circular tower of which only the foundation course remains.

Sacsahuaman was a holy place, for it marked the final wall against which the Chanca power was broken in the terrible days when Inca Yahuar Huaccac had to be killed because of his defeatist policy, and his valiant successor Viracocha Inca had to win back the land around Cuzco and create an empire anew. The work at Sacsahuaman is stupendous because it was made to resist even the threat of another uprising of the subject tribes. Its enormous stones are of local rock polished into polygonal shapes which fit each other without leaving space for levering them apart. With its re-entrant angles and redoubts, and fighting platform path within each ring of walls, it could have withstood any force in the world at the time. When eventually the Spaniards saw it the true Inca was dead and the usurper Atahuallpa was their prisoner. It saw some fighting during the Inca

101

Sapa Inca Huayna Ccapac going to war

102

Inca nobles building Sacsahuaman

The fortress of Sacsahuaman

revolt, but there was then no devoted garrison fighting for a duly ordained Sapa Inca and the brave resistance was of little effect.

Sacsahuaman was an Inca fortress *par excellence* and it was unique. There were many other fortresses, including the great Paramonga, built like a terraced mountain of adobe bricks, which guarded the Chimu kingdom until it fell to Inca storm troops. Elsewhere the Inca were pressing outwards and they usually fortified border areas after conquest. Where there were local resistance fighters the aim was to sweep past them and then to invest their fortresses for storming at leisure if they still refused to accept the divine clemency offered by the Child of the Sun. If they were captured the leaders might be made into an example like the Cara generals who were made into drums for a great festival. They were killed and their intestines ripped out. Then the bodies were carefully dried to remain as lifelike as possible and the abdominal skin was fitted over a bentwood frame in the cavity. They were then slung on a carrying frame and beaten as drums. Perhaps they were not very musical, but they had a definite amusement value to the people who liked to laugh at the fools who resisted the Sapa Inca, and they were a neat piece of propaganda to put the idea of peaceful submission simply and clearly to visitors from neighbouring tribes. But usually dissident warrior chiefs found it convenient to submit and enjoy the very real improvements which came in with Inca rule.

Topa Inca Yupanqui receiving the head of an
enemy chief

The campaigns which Topa Inca Yupanqui led in Chile were marvels of organization. Dried mummies of people who died on the march are still occasionally found with the wood and clay vessels used in life around them. The road lay through the mountains and there was a less carefully marked track along the coastal desert. The two roads were necessary even though the mountain trail, where there were few local people to help, had to be prepared by a specialized engineering corps. They not only prepared the track but also swung giant suspension bridges into place where necessary. One must remember that even when bundles of osiers had to be carried to plait into the suspension cables, they were carried on the backs of men. There was no wheeled transport and the eight-miles-a-day pace of the little llama with its load of sixty pounds was of no use to an army. As the mountain road came near its objective the bulk of the army marched down trotting their regular twenty miles, or a little more, each day. Another army came along the coastal track with extra supplies brought for them on balsas. Then at the point where all met on a front across the country from mountain to sea they could sweep forward to the Maule river and mop up at leisure all the fortresses which they had bypassed.

An assault on a fortress was begun by the slingers. They were very accurate, and their sling bolts could pierce the best Peruvian helmet with ease. They were of little use against the quilted war coats and shields, but they could inflict casualties on any visible head and dispose of the lightly clad slingers on the side so that the assault troops could move up. Fortress walls were rushed and often feints were employed to get the defenders away from the point of main attack. The higher walls were stormed by soldiers who formed into human pyramids so that the warriors could climb quickly over their backs to set about the defenders with their deadly maces. Defence was usually by long spears as well as sling shots, but once the walls had been occupied there was little hope of further resistance. Prisoners were roped together, and, very rarely, a few were sacrificed in thanksgiving to Viracocha and the Sun. Mostly they were detained until they could be put back in their villages and made to work in the Inca fashion with a military garrison nearby to make certain that pacification was complete. It was quite rare for the captives to be made into slave gangs except to bring the local roads and villages up to the standards required by the Inca. Their burden was light, and taxes were deliberately made as small as possible for the first few years until the community had learned the ways of the true civilization of Tahuantinsuyu, in which they were now junior partners.

The army was, as we have seen, mostly a selective service draft. Part of the plan was to use the periods of service to find men who were temperamentally fitted to form the nucleus of the army as specialists in the trades which had to be carried out to a high degree of perfection. Builders, stone masons, bridge experts, skilled assault leaders, were all key men. If other considerations permitted, they were encouraged to remain in the army; but problems in their home region might demand that they were returned to civilian life. Another special consideration was that when there were wars to be fought the army was selected from members of tribes as far as possible from the area of the struggle. This was to prevent fraternization, and also to save young men from having to fight against people whom they may have known in the markets at home.

In this way feelings were spared, and also young men were taken on the march to see the immense extent of their country. When they were old on the farms they told of their

EL SETÍMO CAPITÃ
INGA·MAITAC·

ýdolo uanco

pucara
fortaleza

andamarca y lucana
parinaco chas soras
poma tan bos condes
chyangas yungas—

ynga

Assault on a fortress

CONQVISTA
LEVĀTOSE·PO·RREI·Ī
GA·MANGO   INGA

kono yaciento del ynga llama
do·usno·
enchuzio

mangoynga

The Sapa Inca with his war chiefs

108

Plate 14. The buildings known as the Bath of the Inca at Tampu Mach.
near Cuzco. *Photo: George Rainb*

adventures even if they had only served the short term of three or four moons. They might have stayed on their plot all the rest of their lives according to the regulations, but Tahuantinsuyu would remain for ever a reality and a concept for which they had worked and fought. Even for the least member of the army this was an immense cultural advantage. It was probably not worked out scientifically by the Incas, but the army provided the kind of adventure, expansive in space and time, which was right for the male personality as distinct from the female tendency to home making which was supported by the weaving workshops as well as the security of village life.

The demands made upon army commanders were considerable especially because the state organization of roads and supplies made the logistic problems an exact science. The general had a fine service of information about these matters and could calculate just for what period of time and how easily he could move his men across the country. This kind of thing made for a rather calculating and unadventurous type of mind, but the system was planned for a precise method of attack and defence. Adventure was not desired, apart from the personal bravery of individual warriors. The plan was to surround the enemy and offer terms of surrender, and only to fight if necessity demanded. So the exact calculation of risk was an important matter. Numbers of men must be brought to bear against the enemy in a clear superiority, but it was distasteful to waste man-power, so there must be no great excess.

On important occasions the Sapa Inca took personal command of the campaign, as did Topa Inca Yupanqui in his foray to the south. The skill with which it was undertaken serves to show his outstanding ability as a commander. Its scope included a far greater extension of Tahuantinsuyu than any previous war, and it involved problems of state such as the extension of the main highways which would have been beyond the competence of an army commander alone. In this case the Sapa Inca was acting as viceroy of the Sun in extending the national territories. Another group of peoples were to be brought into the beneficial embrace of the Land of the Four Quarters.

That Topa Inca Yupanqui moved south in answer to a specific challenge arising from movement of the semi-civilized Diaguita or Calchaqui tribes of Argentina and Chile is a probability but unproven. The results of the Peruvian victory might well have been an entry of the army into the unused but fertile lands of the pampas and the Chaco, and this would have allowed Tahuantinsuyu to continue expansion in almost any direction without difficulties in the food supply. However, when the boundaries had been established along the river Maule the processes of pacification and assimilation were allowed to proceed naturally without any further war of expansion. Instead the struggles moved to the northern frontier, where tensions were mounting which were to develop into a great war in the reign of Huayna Ccapac, the son of Topa Inca Yupanqui.

Meanwhile on the eastern borders of the forest lands there was continuous skirmishing and trading. The wild tribesmen were few in number and rarely combined for a big raid. But the uncertainty of the situation meant that a constant patrol from garrison forts was a necessity. The soldiers in this hot country were usually chosen from the coastal peoples. They withstood the climate well, but fell victims to the "evil spirits of the forest" who brought strange fevers to kill them. Their science had not discovered that the deadly illnesses came through infection with disease germs from the forest insects. So the forest garrisons were relieved fairly frequently, as it was considered unwise to

ate 15. The Intihuatana (Sun Throne) at Machu Picchu. *Photo: Victor von Hagen*

111

ate 16. The Kenco Stone near Cuzco, believed by the Inca to be the body of a brother of e first Inca turned into a puma-shaped rock by the Sun god. *Photo: Miss G. Farnell*

Chilean Diaguita vase representing a human
figure wearing decorated *cushma* or shirt of
Inca type

subject men to long periods of this unpromising border patrol. There was also an
element of special danger from the wild Indians, who might take a fancy to shoot a
stray soldier dead with one of their long bamboo-bladed arrows. Treachery was also to be
reckoned with, for a small group of primitive traders might suddenly turn to killing
and robbing if there were not enough soldiers immediately present to overawe them.

The Inca power was famed throughout South America. The Spaniards first heard
rumours of the gold-land from the Indians of the Pacific coast of Darien. No doubt the
story had been taken a thousand miles by word of mouth from tribe to tribe, coming
eventually from canoe-using peoples who had seen the great balsa rafts and heard of
distant Inca cities. The story spread from one group to another without any precise
details, and yet there was a rumour so definite that it gave the pointer which eventually
led to the conquest.

A few Spaniards entered Peru as captives from the south-west. They were among
prisoners taken in a battle between the Calchaqui and Spanish ships on the La Plata.
These captives saw the land soon after Topa Inca Yupanqui had brought his frontiers
to the Calchaqui country. Some people say that they introduced domestic fowl, but a
survivor in later years said that fowl were in Peru still earlier. Maybe they were brought
by boat from Polynesia, though this seems doubtful since it would involve contact with
the more distant islands in western Polynesia.

In Inca times Peru was so self-sufficient that there was really little exterior trade. One
can give no rational explanation of the groups of pottery of two different periods which

112

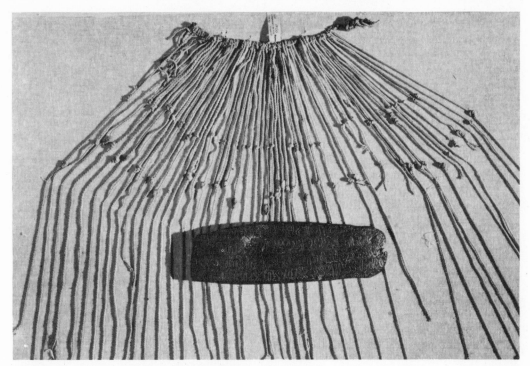

Easter Island wooden tablet and Peruvian *quipu*

Dr Heyerdahl found on the Galapagos Islands. There was no settled human population on the islands, and no reason for pottery to be taken from the northern half of the Peruvian coast for trade to the north, because the only pottery to be found in Ecuador was similar to that already available in Peru itself, and the pottery of the people further to the north was of equal quality, though different in style from Peruvian ceramics. It is of interest that the two groups of pottery from the Galapagos belong to periods when the Peruvians were most active: in the later Mochica times just before the Chimu king Naymlap descended on the coast from a large balsa raft, and in the time of the Inca conquest of the same part of the coast. The only rational explanation would seem to be that we have the remains of shipwrecks which had taken place when sea travel was at a peak, and the vessels had been driven by southerly gales on to the Galapagos. The other explanation, that the pottery vases may have been abandoned by sailors who visited the Galapagos with cases full of curios, is even less satisfactory. One asks, why those periods? And in any case, why abandon expensive curios?

This leads us on to the consideration of transpacific contacts in ancient times. The accounts of voyages of the Polynesians from the Marquesas Islands, as collected by Mr Craighill Handy forty years ago, are as vague and also as definite as the accounts collected by the Spaniards after the conquest about the voyage of Topa Inca Yupanqui. There can be little doubt that two-way navigation was possible. The introduction of the sweet potato, the totora reed, and perhaps the coconut, show that man had a hand in the transmission. The languages of the two races were different, as were their physical types.

If there had been an admixture of cultures, there remain very few visible evidences of it. The Marquesan Islanders transmitted messages on strings, but they knotted symbols like shells and feathers into a single cord and so produced something very unlike the Peruvian *quipu*. The Easter Islanders had a system of writing, in use until at least the late eighteenth century, which was syllabic in construction. Now that it has been translated it proves to be Polynesian, and the chants on the wooden tablets to be typical Polynesian mythological material. Polynesian sails were slung from a single mast and boom, Peruvian sails were slung on a structure not unlike a pair of sheer-legs. But since the Peruvian sails were the only ones known to pre-Columbian America they might have been a local invention inspired by the sight of such things on a big sailing catamaran.

There are enough parallels for one to be sure that there is a problem to be solved about transpacific contact. Perhaps the strangest parallel is the use of a bamboo raft on the coasts of Formosa which is identical in method of construction and which uses the otherwise unique centre-board method of steering found on the Peruvian coast. Unfortunately there seems to be no clear evidence of the Formosan raft being used in the sixteenth or earlier centuries.

The general probability is that both Polynesians and Peruvians knew of the existence of each other. Certainly the Marquesan legend, and the Peruvian one too, state that the navigators were going out to make a planned landfall. This means there had been previous voyages on each side, some of which had returned successfully. We cannot accept that there were any large movements of population, but it does seem very likely that two or three voyages either way might occur within a century, and the probability is that most of them were storm-driven at least in the early stages of the contact.

Thanks to the impetus given to discovery by Dr Heyerdahl, carbon datings have been sought out over the whole of the Polynesian region. The travel of the Polynesian culture-bearers can be traced over nine centuries or more from southeast Asia to the Marquesas. But it is noted that the date of the early charcoal found on the site of fires in a ditch cut across one end of Easter Island is several centuries earlier than would have been expected if the first visitors had been part of the migration of the main body of Polynesian navigators.

One can be sure that this problem was of little consequence to the Inca administration. They obviously knew a good deal about the people to be found on the islands of the great ocean, but the possibility of incorporating such an unusual world in Tahuantinsuyu was even smaller than the possibility of bringing the Amazonian forest tribes into the fold. As we have seen, there is just a suspicion that some people of the Colombian Amazon were descended from early Polynesian *mitimaes*, but there is no historical, or even legendary, account of such a happening. Tahuantinsuyu was apparently a closed community which, like an amoeba, opened its borders only to increase its own unified being. It was, however, a land with a quality of greatness which is reflected for us most strongly by its cultivated taste in the arts and crafts.

Chapter Six

THE HOUSE OF BEAUTY

There are few civilizations which give evidence of an aesthetic sense so uncompromising as that expressed in Inca culture. There is such a uniformity of design in architecture, pottery, woodwork and weaving that one must assume a conscious directing mind of the official classes who controlled production. This mind had some traditional influence from Tiahuanaco, but it developed a power and independence quite its own. This aesthetic is of the highland peoples.

When the Inca power overcame the Chimu kingdom, Inca ideas infiltrated a little in the field of art. Silver and pottery show this more clearly than textiles, because the Inca law decreed that local costume should remain as a mark of the tribal affiliation of the wearers. The silver and pottery so characteristic of the Chimu kingdom assume Inca forms to some extent, but without much feeling. For one thing, the techniques of manufacture were quite different in the two regions; for another, the Inca spirit was not that of the Chimu, and the result of the contact was a catastrophic fall in Chimu standards of design.

One assumes that the Inca officials did not care whether the coastal people produced artistic work or not. Presumably a certain production of Inca style forms for official purposes was all that was required. No doubt the officials were not interested in bringing craftsmen with them. But it indicates also that the Inca aesthetic taste was not a matter which seriously affected official minds when not employed in the highland areas. One can see that it was rooted in tradition. Its extent did not expand to any significant degree after the Inca rule had completed control over the mountain plateaus by the defeat of the Chanca confederacy. In turn we must note that the Chanca peoples were in many ways the cultural heirs of Tiahuanaco, equally with the Inca. There was probably a basic similarity of tradition.

Thus we have an example of a very powerful and well defined aesthetic tradition which was really provincial in distribution and which had its origins in history. There seems no possibility of attributing the style to an innovator, neither can we give a clear date for its full development. It succeeded the style of the Pucara period, which was a debased echo of Tiahuanaco style. Perhaps we should be close to the truth if we said that the Inca aesthetic was crystallized in the late thirteenth century or early fourteenth century and was probably imposed by regulation over the whole of the conquered peoples who had a culture similar to that of Cuzco. One would like to impute it to Inca Viracocha, who not only made the nation into a power but assumed the name of the great spirit himself. But there is in fact no evidence.

We can have no doubt that in Inca times there was a sense of beauty and enjoyment of life. There are no reliable accounts of how people spent their leisure. They seem to have regarded life as a whole without any very definite leisure hours. The view was not a gloomy one. It fitted in with the whole concept of life. From dawn to dusk every member of the family was active and mostly without hurry. There was organization enough to allow of people working together in cultivation or in household tasks.

The frequent festivals and the great ceremonies gave opportunities for enjoyment to all. When travelling or sitting down at home the women would always be spinning thread. Men would be plaiting slings or whittling wood for use. They made many of their own tools, and all the simple furniture they needed. People sang a lot, work songs were rather like play songs, helping to keep a rhythm and so making work easier. One finds an occasional mention of singers, but no description of how they sang and how they became specialized.

One would suppose that an ancient Peruvian would have difficulty in understanding our concept of leisure time. There must have been very little point in trying to be an individual doing things for oneself. The dress and the style of almost everything was prescribed from infancy onwards. The scope for self-expression could only come through doing everything as well and as satisfactorily as possible. This was a trait which would help towards specialization in life. There was a social sanction of approval for capability and good housekeeping, but the person who could succeed through this path to advancement was one who simply had the correct temperament. There must have been a real devotion and artistic quality expressed in such a life.

The development of a conforming personality was the true expression of the culture of ancient Peru. It was a development very strange to the modern individualist. The aim was to become a good citizen working for the Sun, the Sapa Inca, and one's neighbours. It did not involve the separation of the individual from the community. This identification of the self with a kind of greater self, made from the earliest days of life, was probably the reason for the quality of Inca style in art. The buildings are massive, the decorations full of cunningly contrived repetition. It reflects the community and passing events, the aim and its achievement by hundreds of similar actions. This of course reflects the technology, but one must remember that the technology was of little value when compared to the state which it served. The same applied to the relationship between the individual and the concept of Tahuantinsuyu. Here we see the reason for the great division between highland and coastal art in Inca times. The highland people had been conditioned to these styles, and filled with the aspiration towards participation in the state as a portion of a vastly greater whole. The coastal people were used to the idea of a state and organized life, but it was not the Inca state, neither could they make their fingers create Inca design successfully. Their struggle seems to have been directed to the development of an easier life. Their techniques were often advanced. They used moulds for making pottery and seem to have favoured an immense variety of design in their textiles. Their houses were decorated objects, with massive clay walls decorated like textiles as if once they had been simple shelters of matting under the sun.

There was probably a good deal more individuality among the Chimu than in Inca communities. The highlanders charged the coastal peoples with laziness and sexuality. They were shocked by occasional naked ceremonial and by even the small percentage of pottery vessels which represented sexual activities. Yet there is no reason to think that the Inca system disparaged sex or found it wrong. The clash was with the personal expression of emotions. Almost automatically the highland Peruvian mind turned to the safety of formal behaviour patterns, and patterns which were beautiful in simplicity and without disturbing variations and individualities. It is obvious that they tolerated the Chimu customs during the century of domination. But that did not make them imitate them. The Inca aesthetic ran deep in the personality and was not moved.

Today, looking at the art products of the time, one can see that the Inca people were right, even if unconsciously so, for the perfection of their products was incomparably better than those of the coastal people under their domination. One has only to look at the barbarous glory of a late Chimu crown and compare it with the quiet perfect simplicity of an Inca beaker.

To a great extent the concept of art depends upon the presence of an aesthetic standard of judgement. We have no reason for thinking that this was expressed more openly in ancient Peru than by the all too familiar expressions about "the right way" and "the wrong way" of making things. Luckily for the Peruvian artists, this judgement seems to have been based on fitness for purpose. Nevertheless there must have been an extreme dislike of change in such a stable society. There was no chance of experiencing a wide range of art forms from within the culture.

The Peruvians had two distinct interior cultures in Inca times, of which the Inca tradition was dominant, but the Chimu tradition filled a natural place because of its adaptability to the environment.

Contact with other traditions was small and did not present much possibility of influence because surrounding peoples were mostly lower in cultural level. The kingdom of Quito was less centralized than the Peruvian monarchy, but its art traditions were more primitive. Pottery was heavy and uninspired, though it occasionally shows vigorous free-hand modelling. Architecture was simpler. Of the textile arts we have no record, but they can hardly have surpassed the skills of the Peruvian weavers. In metalwork the northern tradition was only a simplification of Inca forms, and did not approach the quality of the still more distant Quimbaya craftsmen of Colombia. From the western forests the Incas acquired feathers, but there was not a great deal of skill in their use among the wild Indians. Some of the border tribes performed masked dances which were much admired as a curiosity by the Peruvian highland people, but there is no tradition of the use of masks by the Peruvians themselves.

The Peruvians may have seen a few examples of the wonderful wood carving of Polynesia, but it is unlikely that they could appreciate its rhythmic qualities which were openly based on the beauty of sex, and so not in accordance with Inca reticence in that matter.

There was simply no way for Peruvian art to move towards new forms and no possibility of an outburst of experiments in new ways of artistic expression comparable to the turbulence which arose in late nineteenth century Europe. In evaluating the quality of ancient Peruvian art we cannot hope to consider it entirely from the Peruvian standpoint. Even the determination of an aesthetic standard is based on our own judgements. We can tell very well what the content was in material forms, but we cannot see it as they imagined it to be. It is, however, very interesting that the basic simplifications in Inca period art can be paralleled today in the *avant garde* galleries of western Europe.

The two great arts in Peru were stoneworking and weaving. All the other arts are

Inca stone bowl with handles in the form of
stylized puma heads

influenced by the forms derived from these two basic crafts. The simplicity of stone-
work was basically due to the techniques used by the masons. The use of stone tools
and sand, for working stones harder than the hammered bronze chisels of Peru, conditioned the broadness of surface design and the nature of the finish applied. Since the
process was laborious and slow, it was an aid to efficiency when the natural forms were
closely followed. In building, less alteration in the natural shape of a block of stone
meant less labour, which could in turn be used in finding another block which, with
minor modifications, could be fitted to the surfaces of the first block.

The close following of natural form brought about an appreciation of shape which
resulted in much beauty. The natural colours and contours of a good stone were little
altered (plate 9), as for example in making stone mortars. In jewellery this principle was
still more important in the manufacture of crystal and turquoise beads. Minor modifications to give a purity of line, and the production of a surface which was glossy without
being glassy were the products of technique in the first place, and probably had a quality
of acceptability rather than the aesthetic appreciation which we give to them today.

But with some rocks no effort was spared to give the exact form intended by the
craftsman. These seem often to have been of homogeneous consistency, like the plain
grey basalt, but some marbles in which natural banding was accepted as an element in
design were worked in this way. In these cases the forms were cut with great accuracy,
and edges made as clean and sharp as was possible with the tools available. A small stone
bowl treated in this way will be a clean and well proportioned object which falls among

118

Inca stone bowl in the form of a bird

the group of forms related to weaving techniques, and yet shows the quality of the material from which it is made. If a great deal of labour was to be expended on producing an exact shape, it was conditioned to the Inca tradition, and the material was not allowed to interfere in any way. Thus we have two styles, adaptation of natural form, and a lesser group of objects in which traditional design takes first place.

Both groups of objects in stone are within the Inca aesthetic tradition. Once seen they remain unmistakable.

On the coast the traditional arts did not include the creation of large objects out of stone. This was not due to luxury and laziness, vices which the highlanders were always ready to impute to the Chimu people. The direction of Chimu art was conditioned by the plastic arts in the sense that they were influenced by modelling techniques more than by carving. They were, however, as handy with the jeweller's drill and fine abrasives as the Incas ever were. We can tell this from their jewellery. They inlaid turquoise in gold and enjoyed the colder blue sharpness of copper carbonate, but they shaped the metal around the natural forms of the stones after they had been polished. In the years of Inca domination the gold was all taken as tribute for the Sun god and the princes related to the Inca, but there is ample evidence from archaeology that this attitude towards the treatment of stone and gold has roots in the distant past.

Another coastal art, which was appreciated in the highlands, was work in shell. The design of shell beads was conditioned by rectilinear weaving patterns. They were sufficiently soft for one colour shell to be inlaid in another, and for complex patterns to be engraved in small scale without any great difficulty to the skilled craftsman. Round beads were probably derived from sea-worn hinges of bivalve shells, and were mass-

Chimu shell pendant

Inca textile bag showing rhythmical geometric
decoration

produced. The coast provided a pleasing range of white, grey, purple, red and yellow shells, as well as flat shells lined with iridescent nacre.

The Chimu taste tended towards the use of complex bead forms strung as single and double chains. They do not seem to have made any broad bands of beadwork like the Iroquois wampum belts. Banded decoration was more brilliantly produced in textile materials. However, shell pendant fringes were made to give garments a gracious rustling accompaniment to movement, and shell decorative motifs were used stitched on the surface of garments. Fish in two or three colours, or little figures of sea birds, were bored by thin bronze drill points making holes only just large enough to admit a single strand of cotton thread. Shell was also used as an attractive material for direct inlay and for composition as micro-mosaics set in mastic gum for decoration. The attractive shell jewellery was quite acceptable to Inca taste, particularly because the severity of textile design suited the material and fitted in well with Inca geometric taste. It is quite acceptable to modern eyes because of its use of strong form and subtle combination of colour. It opens for us a world of appreciation of delicate nuances of tone, and rhythms of form, which are heightened for us by the association of the material with a world of nature with which our civilization has insufficient contact.

The textile art reached high levels of brilliance in Inca Peru. Our appreciation of its rhythmic qualities and the relationship of colour to space has nothing to do with the ideas of the Peruvians. They were interested in the quality of the material, whether it was cotton, alpaca, or vicuña. This had a social connotation, for the wild vicuña produced the soft and delicate wool which was spun and woven by the Sun Maidens for the garments of the Inca and his nobles, and for gifts to great chiefs. Ordinary llama wool was not used, and the skin of the animals was used for leather, not textile.

The Inca family prided themselves on the delicacy of the finest woven material, called *chumpi*, which was quite specially their own social possession. This material was light and fine, probably not unlike cashmere in quality. It was apparently of rather open fibre which conserved air in the weave and so produced a warm, cellular inner structure which allowed this delicate fabric to be worn comfortably even in the stone palaces of the high plateau, which seem to have had the most inadequate heating systems. The fineness of the spinning, the closeness of the weave, and the accuracy of the pattern were the qualities required by the Peruvians in a woven textile. Their views about pattern were conditioned by an arithmetical aesthetic. The basic chequer-board of Inca style was enriched by abstracted forms which are geometric to us, but to them represented real objects through symbolism. The artist worked on a precise system of permutation and combination of colours, and this was enhanced by double weaves, and damask weaves. It was comparatively simple with a two-colour or two-surface-toned material, but when it came to the use of three or more colours the pattern was often arranged so that each repeating element in the design was depicted in each of the colours in turn. The design was not complete until the whole series of possible combinations of colour had been produced.

Under the Inca the choice of design elements was apparently severely limited, but our knowledge is incomplete in this particular because the Inca textiles of the highlands have not been preserved to anything like the same extent as the products of the coastal workshops. But even on the coast the mathematical concept of excellence was the criterion of art. To our eyes the work has a certain monotony of rhythms, almost like some forms of what is now called "Pop art", and it has impeccable good taste. The colours always harmonize well, and the proportions are very satisfying, but nobody counts the warp and weft threads except in textile museums. However, it was this business of counting and changing colours which created the textiles on the loom and was the basis of appreciation in Peru itself.

The loom in ancient Peru was almost the simplest device of its kind used by humans. It was made simply from two loom bars which were pegged apart while the warp thread was wound on them. Then, when weaving, one bar was hitched to a post or a tree, and the other was rolled into a position where a space for weaving was left in front of the weaver within easy arm reach. This bar was secured by a belt around the weaver's waist. A single heddle was often used, and the spindles were pins with thread wound round them which were thrown from hand to hand as the heddle was lifted or left down to make the weave. As the weaver leaned forward tension was released, as she leaned back the loom tautened. As the work grew she unrolled the warp a little and readjusted her belt. In the end, when the warp was all filled, it was only necessary to cut the ends off the loom bars to have the completed cloth.

Why so skilled a people should not have invented a vertical loom or multiple heddles, or any mechanical device to assist the weaver, is incomprehensible to us. It has become fashionable to say that the Incas were philosophic enough to deliberately seek to make everything by hand because they realized the dangers of mechanical knowledge . . . but that represents the attitude of modern man appalled by the prospect he has opened before himself. The probable truth is that there was leisure and skill sufficient for the textile industry of ancient Peru to continue its own way indefinitely. There was simply no need for any further invention. The means suited the needs and the social system was not strained because people found they could make whatever they needed for home, state and god.

When we look at the textiles recovered from ancient graves we appreciate them in our own way, and admire their quality of design and colour relationships. The methods of weaving determined the varieties of line possible, and within its limitations we are faced by the beauty of rhythmic structure which we are beginning to understand as an aesthetic experience in the visual field.

We have noted that the Peruvian taste in dress was rather limited in Inca times by strict regulations which determined the dress, and in particular the head-dress, of the people of each locality. The importance attached to pattern and colour was greatly magnified. This was the real reason for the care taken in the production of textiles. The dyes seem to have been singularly fast if we are to judge from the brilliant condition of cloth excavated from coastal graves. Cotton itself was grown in two colours, white and cocoa brown, which needed no dyeing.

Fashion was probably almost immutable. The pottery from the coastal regions reproduces human figures, and they show costume for a thousand years before the Inca time. The change in regional costume is minimal over this period. There is no reason to think that there was much more change in the highlands, except that the Inca conquest united many small depressed communities and brought them a prosperity and abundance which had not been enjoyed since the great days of Tiahuanaco and thereby

Inti weeping tears of gold, from the gateway
at Tiahuanaco

improved the quality of workmanship. The figure on the gateway at Tiahuanaco is
dressed in Inca costume to all appearances, except that some of the costume decoration
is different. The real importance of clothing as a means of expression lay in quality and
richness. It was not a particularly graceful costume, and when worn in normal life it
must have presented an almost heraldic appearance, but that was quite in accord with
the Peruvian ideas of personal beauty. The Inca period is notable for its lack of realistic
portraiture, even in pottery. The Chimu never approached the realism of their ancestors,
the Mochica people, who are named after the same Muchik language which was later
spoken in the Chimu kingdom. The physical type of the people did not change, but the
conceptions of art changed from free clay modelling to the more formal approach which
came from imitating metalwork. The concept of beauty was probably important,
although it had more to do with social advancement than love. We hear much from
Spanish chroniclers about the care which the Peruvians took over their personal appearance, and this indicates that the people bothered about beauty. The Ccoya who chose
her maids to be always naked was regarded as an eccentric, but her consideration of
their beauty was quite in keeping with the Inca thought about architecture, and indeed
all forms of art . . . a sense of fitness and perfection in all things.

One of the most perfect expressions of Inca art was pottery. Its form was simple and appropriate, and the aim of the potter seems to have been towards a perfect symmetry. The circular section of the pots is apparently as perfect as if it had been wheel-thrown, but the fact is that it is a little more perfect because the slight deviations from the geometric precision are sufficient to give an impression of greater strength, and smoothness of line. The profiles are shaped by hand, but are adequately symmetrical and very strong. They approximate the forms of stone objects, but have a gentleness of line which can belong only to clay. A particularly interesting feature of Inca pottery is the use of strap handles, made of quite broad bands of clay. They are very practical, but they also have a distinctive visual quality which makes them a strong integral part of design and not mere handy appanages. The painted surface decoration is basically geometric, and not more than three colours are used. The total effect is always of well-proportioned ornament which expresses a quality in the form beneath it. But it should always be realized that Inca pottery and its decoration have basic design relationships with their stone work and textiles. It was an expression of the cultural unity of the highland peoples.

The completely different ceramic techniques of the coastlands only rarely imitated Inca forms. They were concerned with vases which had strap handles so that they could be threaded over a belt, or with double bodies joined by a tube. Many of the vases were further embellished by the sonic attraction of a whistle, usually concealed in a small figure on one of the spouts. The whole of the ceramic tradition was based on metalwork. Even the relief ornaments on the side of the vases appear to have been moulded from repoussé metal bowls. Usually these patterns are based on the design of the contemporary woven textiles.

The whole of the coastal attitude towards art and design differs from that of the Inca culture of the highlands. It is more decorative, with a more rapid rhythmic structure in design, and a much greater sense of lightness. This applies even to wood carvings, and such small things as the beads which were used as weights on the tapestry needles. One cannot escape the feeling that this has a relationship to the maritime life of the Chimu civilization. Everything depended on the sea and its plentiful supplies of food. Water was important inland where the rapid streams from the mountains were used for desert irrigation. Everywhere food and water were connected. Hence the insistence of wave forms, of rapid rhythmic variation, and the symbols of birds and fish used everywhere in the art works. This was the universe of Pachacamac, and it had a sense of teeming life, quite different from the majestic world of the high plateaus which were the home of Inca culture.

There is a certain weakness in Chimu design, almost as if they had succeeded too well and found a way of producing useful things with a simple quick slickness of touch. One can well understand the Inca feeling that the coastal people were frivolous and decadent. They differed from the Incas in just that kind of way. Nevertheless they had made a great achievement in human civilization by creating self-sufficient city units in the inhospitable coastal deserts of Peru. The whole of their condition was different from that of the highlanders and their aesthetic was equally part of their character.

The Incas and later the Spaniards found that the Chimu people had curious sexual customs which they viewed with disdain: the Incas because they regarded them as

Two coastal figure vases with strap handles

unworthy of a people conditioned to the monolithic perfectionism of their own social structure; the Spaniards because of the strains which occurred between their religious beliefs and their animal instincts. This made for a neurosis expressed through rigorous self-discipline and outbursts of fantastic cruelty.

The truth about the coastal people of Peru is that they lived in a tropical climate with many austere features imposed by nature. They therefore found release in a certain gaudiness in art, and an indulgence in sex which, if not statistically excessive, was still too exciting to be faced by the puritan invaders of their country.

This attitude to the emotional life had a great influence on the social life of Peru. In the highlands the comparative limitation of conscious life drove the personality to develop less conscious drives. There appears to have been a kind of general regression into the unconscious. The outer life went on successfully, and there were enjoyments, though of a formal variety. When the opportunity arose for escape it only produced a strange kind of apathy. The *coca* habit was a welcome help for those who wished to enter into the world of semi-consciousness. Even the festival drinking bouts did not release wild physical activity, but sent people into a quiet stupor. The denial of access to this stupor when the *chicha* supplies were cut produced the discontent which even threatened the state in the reign of Topa Inca Yupanqui.

Psychologically the civilization of Inca Peru is very interesting just because of this mass subversion of the individual ego. Development of consciousness hardly began before the person was made part of a system. The ego did not wither away when the discovery of the persona was reached in mature age; it never properly developed. This state of mind did not lead to unhappiness. The rare individuals who developed in a way which we should think normal soon rose above the general level and were selected for positions of responsibility. The mass of the people, however, had no wish to be more than part of the nation. Their life in the haze of the common unconscious seemed natural and right enough. The great power of the Inca period artwork and its uniformity throughout

Plate 17. Minor arts of the Inca: bag for holding crushed *coca* leaves for chewing; carve wooden box to hold a woman's sewing and embroidery materials; bronze staff head wit a pelican; bronze club head with projecting blade; and an instrument with tw knife-blade ends for carving. *British Museum. Photo: Derrick E. Wi*

the highlands reflects this basically primitive psychological state of a population which had made few steps towards individuation.

The coastal population had a different psychological experience. This was expressed by their brilliance in art, and also by weakness in constructional work. Their contact with the highland culture, which was so overpowering, must have led to a loss of ability, and their workmanship shows this.

It was in this coastal region, however, that the Spaniards encountered a reception of quiet non-action. The Inca power lost its spiritual basis in the civil war caused by Atahuallpa's revolt. Yet there was no longer any will among the coastal people either to revolt to form a renewed Chimu kingdom, or to assist the Spaniards actively against Atahuallpa. On the highlands the armies and crowds of citizens had accepted Atahuallpa only in so far as they felt that the power had been given to him by the gods. When he was captured nothing could be done, his lack of divine protection was obvious. Later on the gallant younger leaders of the Incas revolted, but they were doing something new and could not sway the people to follow them. The mass of the highland people were not interested in independence or change. The new gods had taken over.

How the psychological conditions were reflected in literature we do not know. There are a few legends of gods, the romantic play *Ollantay*, and several poems and hymns, but they do not give us any adequate idea of the immense oral literature which once existed. The things which did not interest the Spanish conquerors of the country were simply never written down. The painted boards which contained the history of the Incas were lost, so we have no clue to how far the written traditions coincided with the old knowledge. One can surmise that much beauty and pictorial imagery existed in all the lost literature. This would be characteristic of the dream world of a people living a quietly satisfied life. The literature would have qualities of rhythm and directness of expression which are common to all orally transmitted traditions. The Quechua language developed considerable beauty. It was rich in expression, clear in grammatical construction and euphonious. Quechua was more than the dialect of a governing class: it became an international *lingua franca* which perpetuated itself largely through the constant and exact repetition of traditional tales and poems. A similar phenomenon of language was met with among the Maori of New Zealand, and just the same kind of thing once kept the standards of the bardic traditions of Britain in pre-literate days.

Of ancient Peruvian music there is little to say except through specialist studies. There is some dispute as to whether the music was truly pentatonic, or whether it was based on a sixteen-note scale. A good deal of folk music from the highland areas is probably descended from Inca music. The instruments which survive from ancient times mostly come from the coastal region. They consist of cane and pottery panpipes, rattles, trumpets, whistles, and tambours, of which usually only the wooden frames survive. The Spaniards noted the sadness of the music, but, judging from European music of the sixteenth century, this may have referred only to softness and unusual rhythms. In any case, they can have had little opportunity to hear the joyful hymns to the return of the Sun on the great festival in Cuzco, or the singing of a victorious Inca army. Nearly all of the Inca music is lost to us. The folksongs were always folksongs, and in spite of their charm give us no more idea of the fullness of Inca musical tradition than a little farm-house on the plateau can represent the glory of Ccoricancha.

late 18. The coastal desert, green from irrigation. In the foreground are the
ruins of the great temple at Pachacamac, built on a pyramidal base of adobe (mud
brick). In the distance the misty atmosphere is due to the cold Humboldt Current of
the Pacific washing the hot desert shores. *Photo: Stephen Harrison*

The decapitation of Inca Atahuallpa after his murder

From the technological point of view nothing was made badly in ancient Peru. On the coast much design was inadequate and badly formed, to our eyes. To the Chimu people the change was probably felt to be a refinement towards a new ideal, fitting in with the Inca control of the country. It is hard to imagine them expressing any dissatisfaction with the change of power, yet we can see clearly that from our point of view there was an inadequacy in their design after the conquest of their country. It was probably more due to a conscious attempt to emulate the conqueror, than to an unconscious resistance which led to artistic decline. In fact there is no reason to think that there was any conscious loss, since the attempt was a deliberate move to unite all styles of art within the metal techniques. Within these techniques there was an equally deliberate aim toward abstraction and simplification. Straw-like limbs and sack-like bodily forms probably represent a coastal fashion, not unlike those postwar fashions in European art where unconscious reactions drove artists towards types of form which denigrated the factual shape of humanity. Probably the Peruvian example was generated at a far deeper level since it was accompanied by a real weakness of design and failure to understand the true nature of the materials involved.

The Inca tradition itself just could not collapse in the way that brought the failure of Chimu art. Its final decline took a long time and reflected the social breakdown of the villages, but in the first four centuries after the Spanish conquest the degeneration of Inca art was of the same order as the breakdown of Tiahuanaco culture in the four centuries which were succeeded by the Inca revival.

Pre-Inca pottery panpipes and flute with
Inca bone flutes

Manifestations of national artistic expression were deep matters without locally differentiated variations. Local life was fully cared for at the conscious level through village and town communal entertainment. The plays and festival dances may have been highly formalized, but they were manifested as the activity of a local community. The sense of local unity was strongly emphasized by the regulations about the wearing of distinctive head-dresses. There was every incentive for groups to consider themselves as "we" in distinction from neighbouring groups. A great deal of conscious and well-planned effort went into proving that in every activity "we" were more efficient than "they". That in our time we can distinguish few local traits in Inca period work has no relation to the ancient communal feeling of difference. One can discern exactly the same thing in communities today.

There is nothing that one can add to the description of Inca Peru except to note that it was completely acceptable to its people, and that the resistance to Inca power came mainly from powerful tribes threatened with the loss of their national identity when they were engulfed by Tahuantinsuyu.

The simple fact is that absorption into Tahuantinsuyu was an excellent thing. In every way standards of living and the safety of the individual citizen were promoted. The routine of food growing and house building was more organized and the labour was not increased. Greater tribute was taken by the state, but the improved facilities made up for it in greater production. When a tribe was absorbed the yoke was deliberately made light. Peace descended on the people. It was not an enforced peace but was very much desired.

A problem which is important to us today is to discover what happens to the psychological condition of people in times of peace. But the Inca civilization does not answer that question in our terms. This was a unique culture, and its people reacted in a unique way. The Inca empire was in its beginning not unlike a Sumerian city-imperium of four millennia earlier, but it enlarged and developed into something much greater, and without any significant local competition until its very end.

Chapter Seven

THE INCA AND TODAY

What do we do with the Incas? They have passed into a limbo of history, without any obvious developmental links with the high civilizations of today. Their buildings have become the foundations of modern houses. One of their roads has in part become a section of the Pan-American Highway. Their woodcarving and pottery are fetching moderate prices in the antique markets, but their gold, where it survives, is worth a king's ransom, just as it was when the usurper Atahuallpa was cheated for the gold of Ccoricancha, and died quietly because he was garrotted.

In spite of many currently expressed opinions, the Inca civilization was not totally destroyed at the Spanish conquest. Inca noblemen married into Spanish families, Inca princesses became mothers of Spanish grandees, who were honoured because of their noble descent on both sides. At the viceregal court in Lima the members of the great Inca families attended official functions dressed in an adaptation of Inca costume until the eighteenth century. The Sapa Incas were no longer there; they died when Huascar was murdered, and again when the brave war chief Inca Roca died after the insurrection against the Spaniards. But the Inca family was still there, and also the Indian tribes who had once obeyed every order of the Inca nobles. The worst evil that befell them was the collapse of organization.

The invading Spaniards still following the advanced Iron Age culture of sixteenth century Europe lived under a feudal system where peasants were dependents of land-owning responsible masters. It was a good system in many ways, but it had no contact with the enormous organization of social welfare under the Inca. Roads were neglected under local landlords; the peasants were no longer part of the state and they worked for Spanish lords who thought only in terms of local tribute and not of the welfare of Tahuantinsuyu. Village life continued, but the intimate linkages between town and village as part of a unified society were no longer in existence.

Under feudal conditions the economy ran down gently but certainly. Misunderstandings between the races slowly separated them. The decay became rapid and tragic when the viceroys of Peru were harassed by constant demands for tribute from the decaying Spanish kingdom. The pressure was passed on to the peasants by the landowners. Peasants were treated more and more as serfs, and the standards of life in the neglected villages sank to a misery of poverty reminiscent of some of the most horrible tragedies of war-devastated countries in our own time . . . only in Peru it lasted for a full century.

It is only in the last generation that the Peruvian nation has begun to rehabilitate the remaining three millions of the Indian population. The past losses through general degradation with the concomitant illness and lack of medical care, encouraged by the apathy due to the ancient addiction to *chicha* and *coca,* were terrible. The Inca world

Huaman Poma and his parents at church

CONQVISTA
PRIMERAVITODEES
PANA·QTRAJO·ENLACONQVISTA

Spanish grandees

finally sank in the tragedy of Spain and the internal dissensions of the Peruvian Republic. Only the modern organization of the Peruvian state will be able to rescue the Indians as part of a re-created nation.

The statement of the end of the Inca culture arouses us to speculation. We are presented with the historical fact of two incompatibles which did not follow the usual process of coalescence to produce a new united culture within a few generations. Why did this tragedy occur in Peru? What was the nature of the differences between the two cultures?

The answer is an incommensurable factor, time. The difference in quality of the two cultures, although they met face to face, was of the nature of three thousand years. The Peruvians had reached the Bronze Age; the Spaniards were far away from their own bronze culture which had flourished and fallen before Rome was born. They had gone through developments which gave them horses and iron, and developed a sense of feudal reciprocated responsibilities. Yet in the comparable periods of the Bronze Age few other peoples in the world had reached the Peruvian level of culture. The possibility of high civilization was missed by Europeans in the Bronze Age because of their very quality of individuality. They formed into warring cliques, each band of warriors gathering around a chief and building a fortress from which they raided their neighbours until a stronger power overwhelmed them and taught new ways.

The Peruvians developed at a quite different rate from the peoples of the Old World. They were producing their own foodstuff by cultivating quinoa and potatoes, and, later on, maize, just as early in time as the peoples of the Middle East developed wheat and barley and oats. Fine stone buildings appeared as early as 1600 B.C. at Kotosh, but it is only as late as about 900 B.C. that a high civilization, first appearing in Peru around Chavín de Huantar in the valley of the Marañon, penetrated to the coastlands around the site of Cupisnique. This was only a generation after the death of Solomon, King of Israel. We have no clear idea where the impetus to develop stone sculpture and to make elaborate pottery had its origin in America. The fact that in the south of Mexico there was a very similar development very close in time suggests that the impetus may have come from the Mediterranean to the Caribbean, but alternatively it might have travelled by sea from Chou China to Peru. In neither case, if the impetus really came from outside, were any of the Old World food plants introduced, nor methods of writing nor of working bronze.

This early Peruvian culture seems to have developed a rich later flowering on the coast around Nasca in the south, and influenced the tribes right across the mountains on the edge of the forest.

A quite separate culture arose on the northern half of the Peruvian coast, and it was within this Mochica culture that the use of metals really developed beyond the gold-working of the old Cupisnique people.

It was not until the eighth or ninth century A.D., when Spain was mostly under Arab domination, that a truly unified empire arose in Peru. This centred around Tiahuanaco in Bolivia and spread over the greater part of the country except in the extreme north. It broke up in the eleventh century, and the northern coastal people under northern influences built the rich Chimu kingdom on the ruins of their Mochica culture.

As we have seen, the Inca arose in the eleventh century and re-unified the country in the fourteenth, extending the boundaries of their advanced Bronze Age civilization. They had no horses, and no knowledge of iron or the wheel. This may well have conditioned them towards perfecting human social organization. It was through the planned use of military man-power that they overcame the resistance of all the surrounding tribes and kingdoms.

The deadlock of equally balanced power which characterized the European Bronze Age did not long survive in Peru. It may well be that the difference lay in the European possession of horses and cattle with wheeled carts. The mobility of forces and supplies tended to keep the tribes in about equal balance. Strategy was limited, and indeed drawn out into battles of champions of the types described in the *Iliad*. This could never happen in the pedestrian world of Peru. Command belonged to the organizers appointed by the Inca. At first strategic skill was of primary importance, but later the mere weight of numbers made the forces of Tahuantinsuyu practically irresistible until the myth of the sun king was exploded from within.

Huayna Ccapac, the son of Topa Inca Yupanqui, had to decide whether his sun dynasty was the only power. To have given power to Atahuallpa, his son by a Cara princess, was to deny the belief in the supremacy of the sun king for whom the kingdom was created, yet he divided the imperium between Huascar Inca and Atahuallpa. Having acquired two separate heads, the centralized power lost its initiative. Competition between individual leaders broke out, and the spoils went to the leader who commanded the most effective military organizers.

At this point the enormous power of Tahuantinsuyu broke and fell into the competitive state of the Bronze Age chieftainships of prehistory in the European field. It was impossible for it to go on any more whether the Spaniards had arrived or not. Competition for power had opened on the human level.

Through the debacle we can realize the true nature of what had gone before, the very thing which had made Tahuantinsuyu a reality. It was simply the inviolability of the holy Sapa Inca, and this was the fruit of faith. Everybody accepted his divine kingship. The idea survived its early struggle when the Inca family council deposed Yahuar Huaccac and called his successor Inca Viracocha. From that definition of the support of the Great Spirit, the Creator and Preserver of all mankind, for the Children of the Sun they had no retreat, and there was no need of retreat because the acceptance of the belief was followed by victory and real material progress.

The welfare aspect of Inca rule was important, but it was not in any sense a democratic movement. The statecraft of the Inca family supported the theory that the divine Inca must really act as a father to his people, to shower blessings like the Sun. This idea is of the essence of American Indian chieftainship from its democratic beginnings and long after it had developed a hereditary nature. The feeling of interdependence between chief and tribesmen was strong and natural among the tribes. Whether the original members of the Inca family came from the forests or inherited their pretensions from the rulers of Tiahuanaco, they must have begun with the idea of tribal unity of interest clearly in their minds.

The development of the fantastic unity of art and craft under the later Incas was something unique, yet it should be pointed out that it bears some resemblance to the European development of Gothic art within western Christendom. This ecclesiastical art belonged to the religion and spread from town to town, becoming exquisitely beautiful in its expression of growth and life. It found its unifying factor in the mobility of religious craftsmen who were considered to be exempt from secular power. In the Inca case there was no difference between the secular arm and the religious leadership. The high priest was only the minister of the god who was symbolized by the living holiness on earth of the Sapa Inca.

This state of affairs went beyond the intellectual level; it was connected with deep-seated archetypes within the individual psyche. Every Peruvian was, like ourselves and all other people, disposed to see a symbol of immense potency in the sun. The Inca family were related to this symbol by a physical sexual relationship. The very facts of life linked naturally with the theology and produced a state of mind where the Sapa Inca must have been like a manifestation of the *Persona* in all his terrible strength and completeness. It is hard for anyone in the world of today to understand this state of mind. We look on intellectual understanding much more clearly than the ancient Peruvians. If, in our present time, a small group of people acted in daily life on such an inspiration they would immediately be labelled religious zealots or lunatics: but in Peru it seems to have been a perfectly natural and normal thing to link the Sun and the Inca as a visible manifestation of the completeness of being, transcended only by Viracocha, the First Cause.

In such a state of nearly perfect psychological unison there was great content, even happiness. The efficiency was phenomenal, the expansion in space steady, but the cultural advancement was practically nil. In the best of all possible worlds, where could one find any reason for doing anything differently from the best of all possible ways? Pangloss would have been a truly natural and contented individual in Tahuantinsuyu, having no need to avoid contradictions. Within its frames of reference, Tahuantinsuyu was complete.

The frames of reference in Peru, however, did not include iron, horsemen, feudalism, or private property. The Spanish invasion was totally incommensurable with Tahuantinsuyu. What survived from the ancient ways was due to the Spaniards being sufficiently human to dress up the strange ways of Inca life in a sixteenth century Spanish dress. The divine Sapa Inca was an emperor. His cousins were grandees. The small farmers on their andenes were peasants. Don Quixote de la Mancha was not the only Spaniard who created a world to suit his heart's desire.

The first conquerors from Spain were rough men seeking lordships and fortunes. They arrested, impeached and executed each other, seeking gold for personal gain. The Indian scholars must have despised them as much as did the later Spanish governors. Yet among this mixed crowd there were men sufficiently cultured to see the Peruvians as possible friends, and even to found successful families with Peruvian wives. It is mostly from their children that we hear of the glories of the Inca world. But already by the first generation everything was altered and a glamour had taken over for romance, even true romance, the mighty fact which once was Tahuantinsuyu.

BIBLIOGRAPHY

Baudin, Louis. *A Socialist Empire: The Incas of Peru*. Princeton, N.J., 1961

Hyams, Edward, and Ordish, George. *The Last of the Incas*. London, 1963

Joyce, Thomas Athol. *Archaeology of South America*. London, 1912

Kubler, George. *The Art and Architecture of Ancient America*. Pelican History of Art, Harmondsworth, 1962

Mason, John Alden. *The Ancient Civilizations of Peru*. Pelican Books, Harmondsworth, 1957

Prescott, William H. *History of the Conquest of Peru*. 2 vols, New York, 1847, and many later editions

Steward, Julian H. (editor). *Handbook of South American Indians*. Smithsonian Institution, Bureau of American Ethnology, Bulletin 143, vols 2, 5, and 6, Washington, 1946–50

Von Hagen, Victor Wolfgang. *The Realm of the Incas*. New York, 1957

ACKNOWLEDGEMENTS

For permission to reproduce copyright illustrations, grateful acknowledgements are made to:

Ferdinand Anton, page 15 *top*
British Museum, pages 29 *top*, 31, 33, 37, 39, 40, 42, 45 *top*, 59, 71, 77, 97, 112, 113, 118, 119, 120, 121, 126 and 131
Stephen Harrison, pages 94 and 104
Victor Wolfgang von Hagen, pages 15 *bottom*, 88 and 93

The endpapers are from a photograph by Victor Wolfgang von Hagen.

The drawings on pages 9, 13, 21, 22, 24, 25, 27, 29 *bottom*, 41, 44, 45 *bottom*, 49, 51, 53, 56, 66, 67, 76, 78, 80, 81, 83, 84, 87, 90, 99, 100, 102, 103, 105, 107, 108, 130, 134 and 135 are from the manuscript of Don Felipe Huaman Poma de Ayala and are reproduced by kind permission of the Institute of Ethnology of the University of Paris.

The map on page 12 was drawn by Joan Hardman.

INDEX

The page numbers in *italic type* indicate illustrations